READING/WRITING COMPANION

Mc
Graw
Hill
Education

Cover: Nathan Love, Erwin Madrid

mheducation.com/prek-12

Copyright © McGraw-Hill Education

Send all inquiries to:
McGraw-Hill Education
Two Penn Plaza
New York, NY 10121

ISBN: 978-0-07-901825-0
MHID: 0-07-901825-4

Printed in the United States of America.

4 5 6 7 8 9 LMN 23 22 21 20   B

Welcome to Wonders!

Read exciting **Literature**, **Science**, and **Social Studies** texts!

★ **LEARN** about the world around you!

★ **THINK**, **SPEAK**, and **WRITE** about genres!

★ **COLLABORATE** in discussion and inquiry!

★ **EXPRESS** yourself!

my.mheducation.com
Use your student login to read core texts, practice grammar and spelling, explore research projects and more!

GENRE STUDY **1 BIOGRAPHY**

Essential Question..1

SHARED READ "Irma Rangel, Texas Lawmaker"........................2

Vocabulary/Prefixes and Suffixes..6

Ask and Answer Questions..8

Captions and Timelines...9

Author's Point of View...10

WRITING Respond to Reading...12

Research and Inquiry...13

ANCHOR TEXT Analyze *Elizabeth Leads the Way: Elizabeth Cady Stanton and the Right to Vote*..................................14

WRITING Respond to Reading...17

PAIRED SELECTION Analyze "Susan B. Anthony Takes Action!"............18

Author's Craft: Cause and Effect...21

Text Connections/Research and Inquiry...............................22

WRITING Biography...24

GENRE STUDY **2 FAIRY TALE**

Essential Question..32

SHARED READ "Juanita and the Beanstalk"..........................34

Vocabulary/Root Words...38

Summarize..40

Events and Messages..41

Point of View..42

WRITING Respond to Reading...44

Research and Inquiry...45

ANCHOR TEXT Analyze *Clever Jack Takes the Cake*............46

WRITING Respond to Reading...49

PAIRED SELECTION Analyze "Money—Then and Now"............50

Author's Craft: Voice..53

Text Connections/Research and Inquiry...............................54

Deborah Cannon/AP Images

GENRE STUDY 3 ARGUMENTATIVE TEXT

Essential Question 56

SHARED READ **TIME** **"Here Comes Solar Power"** 58

Vocabulary/Homophones 62

Ask and Answer Questions 64

Headings and Sidebars 65

Cause and Effect 66

WRITING Respond to Reading 68

Asking Questions 69

ANCHOR TEXT Analyze *It's All in the Wind* 70

WRITING Respond to Reading 72

PAIRED SELECTION Analyze "Power for All" 73

Author's Craft: Text Features 75

Text Connections/Accuracy and Rate 76

WRITING Opinion Essay 78

WRAP UP THE UNIT

SHOW WHAT YOU LEARNED

• Biography: "Ruby Bridges: Child of Change" 86

• Fairy Tale: "The Tale of Bunny's Business" 89

EXTEND YOUR LEARNING

• Comparing Genres 92

• Homophones and Homographs 93

• Connect to Content 94

TRACK YOUR PROGRESS

• What Did You Learn? 96

Research and Inquiry 97

 Digital Tools Find this eBook and other resources at **my.mheducation.com**

GENRE STUDY **1 BIOGRAPHY**

Essential Question..98

SHARED READ "Rocketing into Space".............................100

Vocabulary/Greek and Latin Roots..............................104

Reread...106

Key Words and Photographs..107

Problem and Solution..108

WRITING Respond to Reading..110

Research and Inquiry..111

ANCHOR TEXT Analyze *Looking Up to Ellen Ochoa*.......112

WRITING Respond to Reading..115

PAIRED SELECTION Analyze "A Flight to Lunar City".......116

Author's Craft: Imagery...119

Text Connections/Research and Inquiry.........................120

WRITING Research Report...122

GENRE STUDY **2 DRAMA/MYTH**

Essential Question...130

SHARED READ "Athena and Arachne"..............................132

Vocabulary/Root Words...136

Make Predictions...138

Stage Directions and Dialogue......................................139

Theme..140

WRITING Respond to Reading..142

Research and Inquiry..143

ANCHOR TEXT Analyze *King Midas and the Golden Touch*...144

WRITING Respond to Reading..147

PAIRED SELECTION Analyze "Carlos's Gift".....................148

Author's Craft: Problem and Solution.............................151

Text Connections/Research and Inquiry.........................152

GENRE STUDY **3 POETRY**

Essential Question...154
SHARED READ "The Camping Trip"........................156
Vocabulary/Idioms..160
Rhythm and Rhyme...162
Stanzas and Events...163
Point of View..164
WRITING Respond to Reading.................................166
Research and Inquiry...167
ANCHOR TEXT Analyze "Ollie's Escape".................168
WRITING Respond to Reading.................................170
PAIRED SELECTION Analyze "The Gentleman Bookworm"........171
Author's Craft: Word Choice.......................................173
Text Connections/Phrasing and Expression..................174
WRITING Narrative Poem...176

WRAP UP THE UNIT

SHOW WHAT YOU LEARNED
- Biography: "Watching the Stars: The Story of Maria Mitchell"..........184
- Narrative Poem: "The Memory Box".................................187

EXTEND YOUR LEARNING
- Comparing Genres...190
- Idioms..191
- Connect to Content...192

TRACK YOUR PROGRESS
- What Did You Learn?..194

Research and Inquiry...195

 Digital Tools Find this eBook and other resources at **my.mheducation.com**

Lou is helping his town honor its heroes. He is being a good citizen. A good citizen helps people, follows rules, and respects others.

Look at the picture. Talk about how Lou is being a good citizen. Listen closely to what your partner says. Then ask a question to make sure you understand. Write your ideas in the word web.

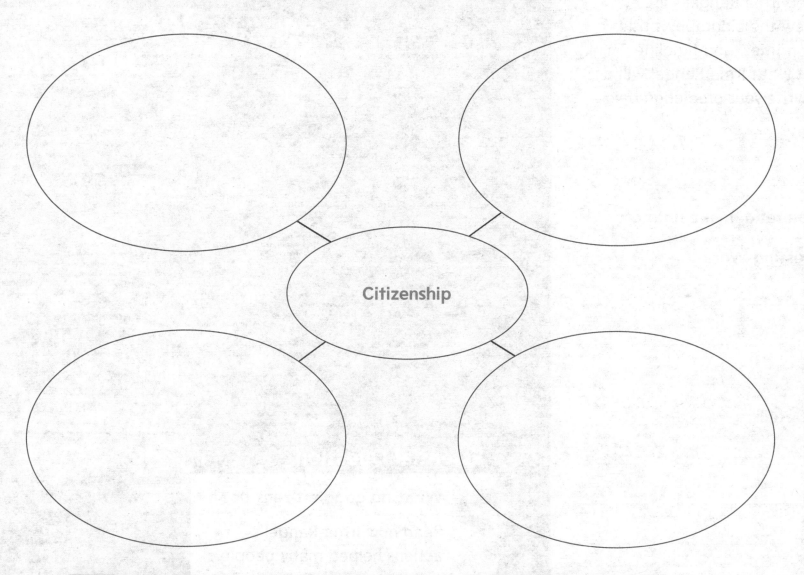

Citizenship

 Go online to **my.mheducation.com** and read "The Generous Grower" Blast. Think about how Johnny Appleseed was a good citizen. Then blast back your response.

TAKE NOTES

To better understand how events shaped Irma Rangel's life, preview the biography's title, section titles, and timeline. Think about what Irma Rangel will do, and write your prediction below.

_____

_____

As you read, make note of:

Interesting Words: _____

_____

_____

_____

Key Details: _____

_____

_____

_____

_____

IRMA RANGEL

Texas Lawmaker

Essential Question

?

What do good citizens do?

Read how Irma Rangel's actions helped many people.

Born in Kingsville, Texas, in 1931, Irma Rangel learned about overcoming obstacles by watching her parents. When she grew up, she used what she learned to help others.

Overcoming Obstacles

Irma's parents never had it easy. Her father lost his parents when he was just five years old. Her mother lost hers when she was 11 years old. They faced **unfairness**. As Mexican Americans, they were not allowed to go to certain schools. They were also very poor, and had to work instead of getting an education.

But they kept a positive attitude, worked hard, and improved their lives. Irma's mother opened her own dress shop. Her father opened his own barbershop.

Irma's mother had a lot of memories of her father. In the late 1940s, a plot of land that she remembered him farming went up for sale. Irma's parents decided to buy it. The neighbors didn't want a Mexican American family moving in, but Irma's parents did not **waver**. They bought the land and built a beautiful house. Eventually, they were accepted.

Irma's parents built a beautiful home on an empty plot of land. In 1951, they moved in and lived there with Irma the rest of their lives.

FIND TEXT EVIDENCE 🔍

Read

Paragraphs 1-2
Author's Point of View
Underline text that shows what the author thinks about how Irma's parents grew up.

Paragraphs 3-4
Ask and Answer Questions
What question can you ask and answer about Irma's parents?

_____

_____

Circle text evidence that helps you answer the question.

Captions
Draw a box around something new you learned in the caption.

Reread

Author's Craft

How does the author help you understand what obstacles are?

FIND TEXT EVIDENCE

Read

Paragraph 1

Ask and Answer Questions

What question can you ask and answer about being a good citizen? Write the question here. **Underline** the answer.

_____

_____

Paragraph 2

Author's Point of View

What does the author think of the fact that few women worked in government? **Circle** text evidence.

Timeline

What year was Irma elected to the House of Representatives?

_____

Reread

Author's Craft

Why is "Good Citizens" a good title for this section?

Good Citizens

The official flag of the state of Texas

Irma's parents believed that good **citizenship** meant helping others achieve success like they had. Her father decided to **participate** in government. He joined organizations that urged people to vote. He got involved in elections by supporting candidates he thought would help people.

Irma's father inspired her. Unfortunately, at the time it was unusual for women to work in government. But Irma was unusually **daring** and risked a lot. She studied law and got a job arguing the government's side in criminal trials. She was one of the first Hispanic women in Texas to hold that job. In 1976 she ran for office and became the first Hispanic woman elected to the Texas House of Representatives.

This timeline shows important dates in Irma Rangel's life.

| 1930 | 1940 | 1950 | 1960 | 1970 | 1980 |

1931: Irma is born

1952: Graduates from Texas A&M University-Kingsville

1969: Graduates law school

1976: Becomes the first Hispanic woman elected to the Texas House of Representatives

Fighting for Fairness

As a Texas lawmaker, Irma worked to help people improve their lives. It **horrified** her that being Mexican American and poor had kept her parents from getting an education. She **proposed** laws that would give all children a chance to learn. One law helped poor students pay for college. Another said that state colleges must accept all Texas students who finish near the top of their high school class.

Irma **continued** to fight for people in need. She worked to defend women's rights and get food to the hungry. To reach her goals, she talked with lawmakers who disagreed with her. But she was never disagreeable. "This is such a good bill," she would tell them. "I know you're going to like it."

Irma's parents taught her how to overcome obstacles. But thanks to Irma, Texans now face fewer obstacles than her parents did. Today, those who work hard find the road to success easier to travel.

(l) Kelly West/AP Images; (r) Paul Iverson/AP Images

1990　　2000　　2010

1994:
Elected to the Texas Women's Hall of Fame

1997:
Named Legislator of the Year

2003:
Irma dies

2006:
Irma Rangel College of Pharmacy opens

Summarize

Was the prediction you made about Irma Rangel at the beginning of her biography correct? Use your notes to summarize the main events of her life.

BIOGRAPHY

FIND TEXT EVIDENCE

Read

Paragraph 1
Ask and Answer Questions
What question can you ask and answer about Irma's work?

_____

_____

_____

_____

Underline the answer.

Paragraphs 2–3
Prefixes and Suffixes
Circle the root word in *disagreeable*. Use its prefix and suffix to write what it means.

_____

Reread

Author's Craft

How does the author help you understand what Irma was like?

Vocabulary

Use the sentences to talk with a partner about each word. Then answer the questions.

citizenship

Planting a tree in your community is an example of good **citizenship**.

What can you do to show good citizenship in your community?

_____

_____

continued

Luis **continued** to read his book all afternoon.

What is the opposite of continued?

_____

_____

daring

It is **daring** to stand up for your beliefs.

Write about something daring you have done.

_____

_____

horrified

Pam was **horrified** when she saw what the storm did to the bird's nest.

What does it mean to feel horrified?

_____

_____

participate

Neena's friends like to **participate** in sports.

What games do you like to participate in?

_____

_____

 Build Your Word List Draw a box around the word _organizations_ in the first paragraph on page 4. Look up the word's meaning using a classroom or online dictionary. In your writer's notebook, write down the word and its definition.

proposed

Dad **proposed** they look online to find the answer to Kia's question.

Write about something you proposed to your family or friends.

_____

_____

unfairness

Our coach discussed the **unfairness** of the referee's decision.

What word means the opposite of unfairness?

_____

_____

waver

Ted's confidence started to **waver** when he forgot the answer.

Describe how you would look if your confidence started to waver.

_____

_____

Prefixes and Suffixes

A prefix is a word part added to the beginning of a word. A suffix is added at the end. To figure out the meaning of a word with a prefix and suffix, find the root word first.

FIND TEXT EVIDENCE

I see the word unusually _on page 4. I find the root word_ usual _first. I know the prefix_ un- _means "not," and the suffix_ -ly _means "in a way that." The word_ unusually _must mean "not in a usual way."_

Irma was unusually daring and risked a lot.

Your Turn Find the root word. Then use the prefix and suffix to figure out the meaning of the word.

unfairness, page 3 _____

_____

Ask and Answer Questions

Ask yourself questions as you read. Then read on or reread to find the answers.

🔍 FIND TEXT EVIDENCE

Look at the section "Overcoming Obstacles" on page 3. Think of a question and then reread to find the answer.

Page 3

Overcoming Obstacles

Irma's parents never had it easy. Her father lost his parents when he was just five years old. Her mother lost hers when she was 11 years old. They faced **unfairness**. As Mexican Americans, they were not allowed to go to certain schools. They were also very poor, and had to work instead of getting an education.

But they kept a positive attitude, worked hard, and improved their lives. Irma's mother opened her own dress shop. Her father opened his own barbershop.

Irma's mother had a lot of memories of her father. In the late 1940s, a plot of land that she remembered him farming went up for sale. Irma's parents decided to buy it. The neighbors didn't want a Mexican American family moving in, but Irma's parents did not **waver**. They bought the land and

I have a question. What did Irma learn from watching her parents? I read that Irma's parents grew up poor, but worked hard and started their own businesses. Now I can answer my question. Irma learned that people can overcome obstacles by working hard.

Your Turn Reread "Fighting for Fairness" on page 5. Think of a question. You might ask: How did Irma help people improve their lives? Reread to find the answer. Then write it here.

_____

_____

Captions and Timelines

"Irma Rangel, Texas Lawmaker" is a **biography**. A biography

- tells the true story of a real person's life
- is written by another person
- includes text features such as timelines, photographs, and captions

FIND TEXT EVIDENCE

I can tell that "Irma Rangel, Texas Lawmaker" is a biography. It includes facts and information about Irma Rangel. There is also a timeline that shows important events in Irma's life in time order.

Page 4

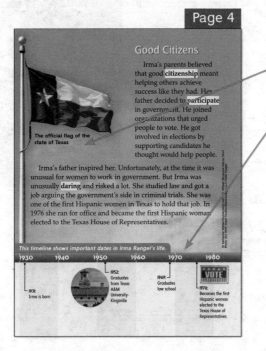

Good Citizens

Irma's parents believed that good **citizenship** meant helping others achieve success like they had. Her father decided to **participate** in government. He joined organizations that urged people to vote. He got involved in elections by supporting candidates he thought would help people.

The official flag of the state of Texas

Irma's father inspired her. Unfortunately, at the time it was unusual for women to work in government. But Irma was unusually **daring** and risked a lot. She studied law and got a job arguing the government's side in criminal trials. She was one of the first Hispanic women in Texas to hold that job. In 1976 she ran for office and became the first Hispanic woman elected to the Texas House of Representatives.

This timeline shows important dates in Irma Rangel's life.

1930 1940 1950 1960 1970 1980

1931: Irma is born

1952: Graduates from Texas A&M University-Kingsville

1969: Graduates law school

1976: Becomes the first Hispanic woman elected to the Texas House of Representatives

Caption

A caption describes what is happening in the photograph. It gives information that is not included in the text.

Timeline

A timeline shows the time order in which important dates and events happened.

Your Turn Look at the timeline on pages 4 and 5. When did Irma Rangel become part of the Texas Women's Hall of Fame? Write it here.

COLLABORATE

_____

_____

Author's Point of View

Point of view is what an author thinks about a topic. Look for details that show what the author thinks.

 FIND TEXT EVIDENCE

When you cite text evidence, you look for text that supports your response. What does the author think about Irma Rangel? I can reread and look for details that tell me what the author thinks. This will help me figure out the author's point of view.

Details
Irma was inspired by her parents to be a good citizen.
It was daring for Irma to run for office.

Author's Point of View

 **Your Turn** Reread "Irma Rangel, Texas Lawmaker." Find more details that show how the author feels about Irma. List them in your graphic organizer. What does the author think of Irma Rangel? Do you agree with the author's point of view?

_____

_____

Details
Irma was inspired by her parents to be a good citizen.
It was daring for Irma to run for office.

Author's Point of View

Respond to Reading

Talk about the prompt below. Think about the author's point of view. Use your notes and graphic organizer.

How does the author help you understand that Irma Rangel is a good citizen?

_____

_____

_____

_____

_____

_____

_____

_____

_____

Primary and Secondary Sources

Primary sources are a great way to learn about the past. A primary source is created by someone who took part in the event. Examples of primary sources are diaries, letters, speeches, and photographs. Personal details in "Irma Rangel, Texas Lawmaker" came from an interview with Irma Rangel. An interview is a primary source.

Secondary sources are created by someone who doesn't have firsthand knowledge of the event. Some examples of secondary sources are encyclopedias and textbooks.

Look at the photograph. Explain why it's a primary source.

_____

_____

_____

Clean Up Our Park

Create a Poster Think of an issue in your local community. Is there a problem that needs to be solved? Read these steps and restate them to your partner. Then create a poster about the issue.

1. Talk with a partner about the problem.
2. Research. Use primary and secondary sources to find out what people are doing to solve the problem.
3. Create a poster that shows the issue. Write a paragraph that describes it.

Elizabeth Leads the Way:
Elizabeth Cady Stanton and the Right to Vote

Literature Anthology: pages 366–383

? How does the author use what Elizabeth says and does to help you understand her personality?

Talk About It Reread pages 370 and 371. Talk with a partner about what Elizabeth Cady Stanton says and does.

Cite Text Evidence What does Elizabeth say and do? Write text evidence and how it helps you understand Elizabeth in the chart.

 Make Inferences

An inference is a guess based on information. What inference can you make about Elizabeth based on the title *Elizabeth Leads the Way: Elizabeth Cady Stanton and the Right to Vote*?

Text Evidence	Elizabeth

Write The author uses what Elizabeth says and does to help me

understand that _____

_____

How do you know that Elizabeth felt strongly about what she believed in?

 Talk About It Reread page 379. Talk with a partner about what Elizabeth thinks about a woman's right to vote.

Cite Text Evidence When you cite text evidence, you look for text that supports your response. What words help you understand how strong Elizabeth's feelings are? Write text evidence in the chart.

Text Evidence	How Elizabeth Felt

Write I know that Elizabeth felt strongly about her beliefs because

the author _____

_____

_____

Quick Tip

I can use these sentence starters when we talk about Elizabeth.

I read that Elizabeth . . .

This helps me understand that . . .

 Synthesize Information

Make a personal connection to what you read about Elizabeth Cady Stanton. Perhaps you have felt unfairness, too. When you make a personal connection to a text, you can deepen your understanding of what you have read.

? **How does the author help you understand how Elizabeth's ideas changed America?**

COLLABORATE

Talk About It Reread pages 382 and 383. Talk with a partner about why the author used the phrase "spread like wildfire."

Cite Text Evidence What other words and phrases show how Elizabeth changed America? Write text evidence in the chart.

Quick Tip

The author uses the phrase "spread like wildfire" to help you picture how quickly Elizabeth's ideas spread.

Text Evidence	What It Means
How It Helps	

Write The author helps me understand how Elizabeth changed

America by _____

_____

Respond to Reading

COLLABORATE

Answer the prompt below. Think about the author's view of Elizabeth Cady Stanton. Use your notes and graphic organizer.

How does Tanya Lee Stone use Elizabeth's biography to teach you about what it means to be a good citizen?

_____

_____

_____

_____

_____

_____

_____

_____

_____

_____

Susan B. Anthony Takes Action!

Literature Anthology:
pages 386–389

1   Susan Brownell Anthony was born in Massachusetts in 1820. Her family believed that all people are equal. At the time Susan was born, however, this idea of equality was very unusual. Men and women did not have the same rights. Women could not vote and they could not own property. Life was different for Susan. She learned to read and write at the age of three, even though she was a girl.

Reread and use the prompts to take notes in the text.

Circle words and phrases that help you understand what equality is. Write what equality means here:

_____

_____

_____

_____

COLLABORATE

Talk with a partner about how life was different for Susan. **Underline** text evidence in the excerpt that supports what you said.

Women Get the Vote!

2   Susan gave as many as 100 speeches around the country every year for forty-five years. She always stayed excited and hopeful about her work.

3   Not everyone agreed with her ideas. Susan and her friend Elizabeth Cady Stanton had to fight hard for many years for the rights of all people. They always did their work peacefully. It was not until fourteen years after Susan died that women in the United States were allowed to vote. The long struggle would not have been successful without the work of Susan B. Anthony.

In paragraph 2, **underline** clues that help you visualize what Susan was like. Write them here:

_____

_____

_____

_____

_____

_____

COLLABORATE

Reread paragraph 3. Talk with a partner about how other people felt about Susan's ideas. What did Susan and Elizabeth do? **Circle** words and phrases that show what they did.

Make a mark beside the sentence that shows how the author feels about Susan.

? **How does the author help you know how she feels about Susan B. Anthony?**

Talk About It Reread paragraph 2 on page 19. Talk about what the author says about Susan.

Cite Text Evidence What words let you know how the author feels about Susan and the work she did? Write text evidence in the chart.

Quick Tip
When I reread, I can use the author's words and phrases to understand her point of view.

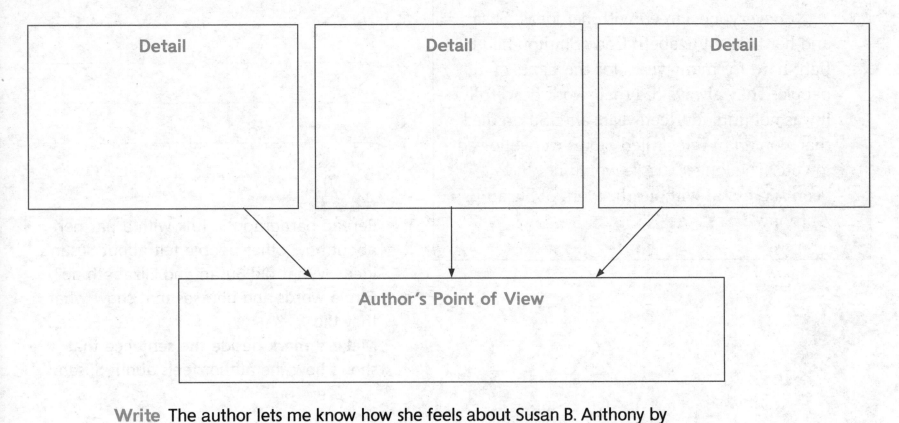

Detail	Detail	Detail

Author's Point of View

Write The author lets me know how she feels about Susan B. Anthony by

_____

_____

Cause and Effect

An *effect* is something that happened. A *cause* is why it happened. Authors often use cause and effect to organize and structure texts. This helps readers understand why events happened.

FIND TEXT EVIDENCE

On page 387 of "Susan B. Anthony Takes Action!" in the **Literature Anthology,** the author uses the words *as a result* to show what happened when Susan's teacher refused to teach her long division.

> As a result, Susan's family took her out of school and taught her at home.

Your Turn Reread the last paragraph on page 387. Use text evidence to answer these questions.

- How do you know what caused Susan to work with Elizabeth?

  _____

  _____

- How does the author's words help you see how Susan felt about

  Elizabeth's work? _____

  _____

  _____

Use signal words to help your readers figure out cause and effect. Some signal words and phrases are: *because, so, therefore,* and *as a result.*

Readers to Writers

Text Connections

? **How do you know how the songwriter of "America" and the authors of *Elizabeth Leads the Way* and "Susan B. Anthony Takes Action!" feel about America?**

Talk About It Read the song lyrics. Talk with a partner about how the songwriter feels about America.

Cite Text Evidence Circle words and phrases in the lyrics that show what America means to the songwriter. Underline what the writer says about freedom.

Write I know how the songwriter and authors feel about

America because _____

_____

_____

_____

_____

_____

_____

Quick Tip

The lyrics help me understand how the songwriter feels. This helps me compare the song to the selections I read this week.

AMERICA

My country 'tis of thee,
Sweet land of liberty,
Of thee I sing.
Land where my fathers died,
Land of the Pilgrim's pride,
From ev'ry mountainside
Let freedom ring.

—Lyrics by Samuel F. Smith

Present Your Work

COLLABORATE

Decide how you will present your poster about a local issue to the class. Use the checklist to improve your presentation.

Save Our Playground!

What Is the Issue?   What's Being Done?

As I practice, I will use the following points to discuss my poster:

_____

_____

I think my presentation was _____

I know because _____

_____

_____

✔ Presenting Checklist

☐ I will make sure my poster is easy to read.

☐ I will make sure everyone can see my poster.

☐ I will look at my audience and not my poster as I speak.

☐ I will speak clearly and slowly.

☐ I will invite questions from my audience.

Literature Anthology:
pages 366–383

Expert Model

Features of a Biography

A biography is a kind of narrative nonfiction. A **biography**

- tells the true story of a real person's life and is written by another person

- is told in sequence, or time order

- can include text features such as timelines, photographs, and captions

Analyze an Expert Model Reread page 381 in the **Literature Anthology**. Use text evidence to answer the questions.

How does Tanya Lee Stone help you understand what happened

after Elizabeth read to the crowd? _____

_____

_____

How does the author use words and phrases to make the biography

more interesting to read? _____

_____

_____

Word Wise

Writers use pronouns such as *he*, *she*, *they*, or *them* to take the place of either singular or plural nouns. For example, the writer of this story says, "They always did their work peacefully." The pronoun *they* stands for Susan and Elizabeth. Pronouns tell the reader whether the author is referring to one or more than one person.

Plan: Choose Your Topic

Brainstorm With a partner, brainstorm a list of people who have been good citizens. Use the sentence starters below to talk about your ideas.

> *A good citizen is . . .*
> *Some things good citizens do are . . .*

Writing Prompt Choose one person from your list. Write a biography explaining how that person is a good citizen.

I will write about _____

Purpose and Audience An author's purpose is his or her reason for writing. Think about who will be reading your biography. That's your audience.

The purpose of my biography is _____

_____

My audience will be _____

_____

 Plan Focus on what you want your readers to learn about the person you chose. In your writer's notebook, write the person's name. Then, draw a Sequence Chart to record the events of that person's life.

Quick Tip

When you brainstorm, you list as many ideas as you can about a topic. Brainstorming with a partner helps you figure out what you want to write about.

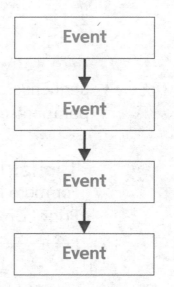

Event

↓

Event

↓

Event

↓

Event

Plan: Research

Use a Variety of Sources You'll need to research the person you chose before writing your biography. Make sure you gather relevant information. Use at least one primary source, and a variety of secondary sources such as books, magazines, and websites. To check that a website is reliable, answer these questions:

- Does it belong to a trusted organization such as a university or respected newspaper?

- Does it offer helpful information such as the author's name, the date the text was written, or links to other sources?

List two sources you will use:

1. _____

2. _____

Take Notes Once you pick your sources, take notes and fill in the Sequence chart you drew in your writer's notebook. Remember to paraphrase, or put the information you find into your own words.

> ## Digital Tools
> For more information about how to take notes, watch "Take Notes: Print." Go to **my.mheducation.com**.

Quick Tip

Remember that a primary source is created by someone who took part in an event. Biographies use primary sources like photographs or quotations. This makes them more interesting to read.

Draft

Sequence Writers often tell the events of a person's life in the order that they happened. This sequence of events helps readers understand what happened and why. Reread this passage from "Irma Rangel, Texas Lawmaker."

Writing a biography in time order makes events more understandable to your reader. It also gives your biography a clear beginning, middle, and end. Words, such as *first, then, next,* and *finally* can help signal the sequence of events in your biography.

> Unfortunately, at the time, it was unusual for women to work in government. But Irma was unusually daring and risked a lot. She studied law and got a job arguing the government's side in criminal trials. She was one of the first Hispanic women in Texas to hold that job. In 1976 she ran for office and became the first Hispanic woman elected to the Texas House of Representatives.

Use the above passage as a model to write about the person you chose by listing important events in time order. Include one date.

_____

_____

_____

Write a Draft Use your Sequence chart to write your draft in your writer's notebook. Remember to use signal words to show time order.

Revise

Quick Tip

Use precise nouns to help your readers visualize people, places, and objects in your biography.

Precise Nouns A noun is a person, place, or thing. For example, *George Washington, Texas,* and *book* are all nouns. Precise nouns are more specific. For example, *science book* is more specific than *book.* Writers make their ideas clearer by using precise nouns.

Reread the first three sentences of *Elizabeth Leads the Way* on page 374 of the **Literature Anthology**. Talk with a partner about the noun *abolitionist*. How does the word *abolitionist* help you visualize what Henry Stanton believes?

_____

_____

_____

_____

Revise It's time to revise your writing. Read your draft and look for places where you might use a noun that is more precise. Circle two words or phrases in your draft that you can change. Revise and write them in your writer's notebook.

Peer Conferences

Review a Draft Listen carefully as your partner reads his or her draft aloud. Say what you like about the draft. Use these sentence starters to discuss it.

I like this part because . . .

I didn't understand the order of events because . . .

Add a more precise noun here to replace . . .

I have a question about . . .

Partner Feedback After you take turns giving each other feedback, write one suggestion your partner made that you will use in your revision.

_____

_____

_____

_____

_____

Revise After you finish your peer conference, use the Revising Checklist to figure out what you can change to make your biography better. Remember to use the rubric on page 31 to help yourself revise.

> ### ✓ Revising Checklist
>
> ☐ Does my biography have a logical sequence of events?
>
> ☐ Did I use at least one primary source?
>
> ☐ Did I use nouns that are precise?
>
> ☐ Are my ideas clear to my readers?

Edit and Proofread

After you revise your biography, proofread it to find any mistakes in grammar, spelling, and punctuation. Read your draft at least three times. This will help you catch any mistakes. Use the checklist below to edit your sentences.

✔ Editing Checklist

☐ Do all the sentences begin with a capital letter and end with the correct punctuation mark?

☐ Do the singular and plural pronouns match their nouns?

☐ Do the pronouns match their relationship to the verbs in the sentence?

☐ Are all the words spelled correctly?

List two mistakes that you found as you proofread your biography.

1. _____

_____

_____

2. _____

_____

_____

Tech Tip

If you wrote your draft on a computer, use the spell-check feature to find any spelling mistakes you made. This feature will offer suggestions to help you spell the words correctly.

Grammar Connections

When you proofread your biography, make sure your verbs agree with your subject. Remember that past-tense verbs describe an action that has already happened. Add *-ed* to most verbs to form the past tense.

Publish, Present, and Evaluate

Publishing When you publish your writing, you create a neat final copy that is free of mistakes. If you are not using a computer, use your best handwriting. Write legibly in print or cursive.

Presentation When you are ready to present, practice your presentation. Use the presenting checklist.

Evaluate Publish, then use the rubric to evaluate your biography.

What did you do successfully? _____

_____

What needs more work? _____

_____

✓ **Presenting Checklist**

☐ Look at the audience.

☐ Speak slowly in a loud voice.

☐ Practice your presentation.

☐ Use a timeline to show the order of events.

4	3	2	1
• describes specific events in a person's life and how they shaped that person • presents events in correct order • uses many precise nouns, and ideas are clear	• describes some important events in a person's life • presents events in correct order • uses some precise nouns, and ideas are clear	• describes a few events in a person's life • some events are out of order • uses few precise nouns, and ideas are unclear	• doesn't give much information about a person's life • events are out of order • doesn't use precise nouns, and ideas are confusing

Talk About It

? Essential Question

How do we get what we need?

lemonade

32

The kids are thirsty. They want a glass of Sue's lemonade. Some will use money to pay for it. Some will barter, or trade. Sue is getting what she needs, too. She is working to save money to buy a new bike.

Look at the photograph. Talk about how the kids in line will get what they need. Write ways you can get what you need in the word web.

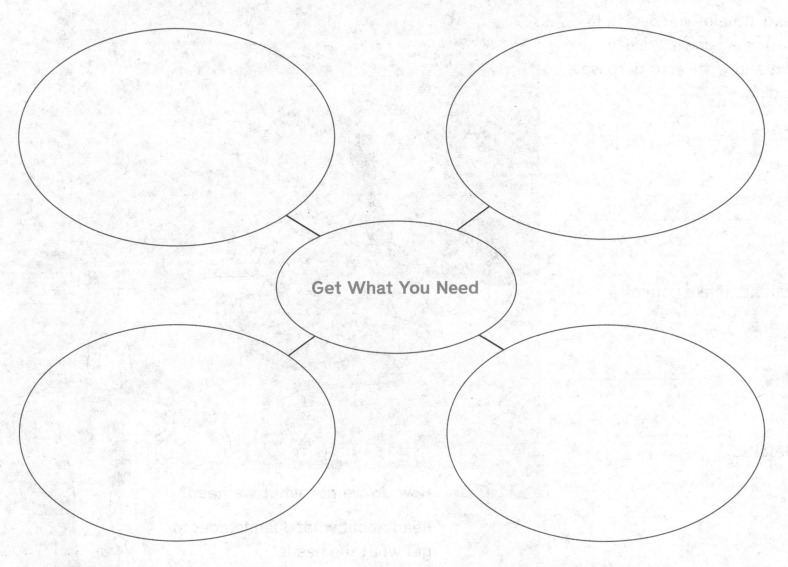

Get What You Need

Go online to **my.mheducation.com** and read the "Strictly Business" Blast. Think about how businesses get what they need. Then blast back your response.

Herman Agopian/The Image Bank/Getty Images

TAKE NOTES

Understanding why you are reading helps you adjust how you read. It helps you decide to reread or slow down. Preview the text and write your purpose for reading.

_____

_____

_____

_____

As you read, make note of:

Interesting Words: _____

_____

_____

Key Details: _____

_____

_____

_____

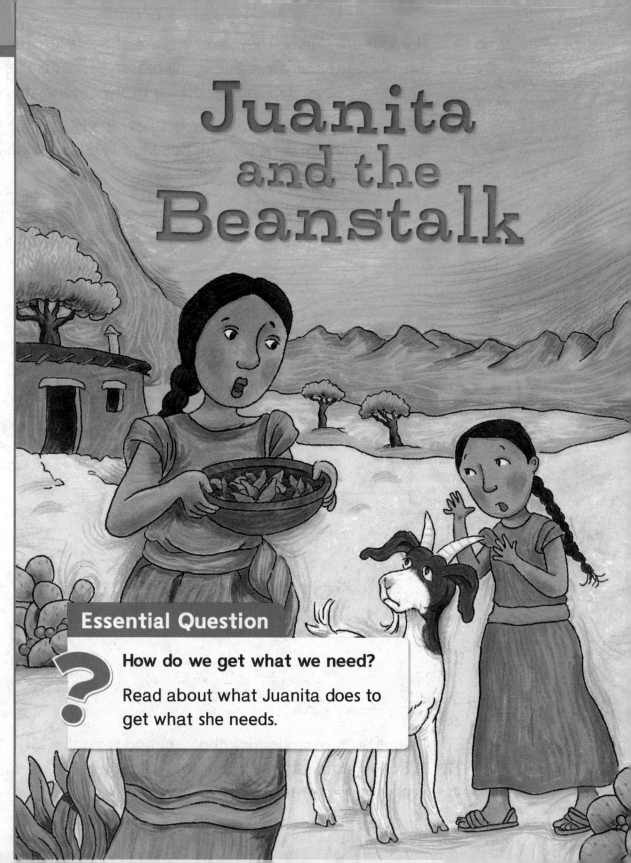

Juanita and the Beanstalk

Essential Question

How do we get what we need?

Read about what Juanita does to get what she needs.

Juanita lived in a small, **humble** cottage with her Mamá and her pet goat, Pepe.

One day Mamá said, "There has been no rain, and our garden has dried up. Juanita, you must go to town and sell your goat. Use the money you get as **payment** to buy some food."

"I don't want to sell Pepe!" cried Juanita. She petted the goat lovingly. But she was an obedient girl and would not disobey her mother. **Reluctantly**, she took Pepe to town. On her way she met an old man who patted Pepe kindly.

"He is for sale," said Juanita with tears in her eyes.

The man replied, "I have no money, but I have some special *frijoles*. If you plant these beans you will never go hungry again. We can **barter**, and I will trade you these beans for your goat."

FIND TEXT EVIDENCE

Read

Paragraphs 1–2

Summarize

What does Mamá tell Juanita to do? **Circle** text evidence.

Paragraph 3

Root Words

Draw a box around *lovingly*. Write its root word here.

_____

Paragraphs 3–5

Point of View

How does Juanita feel about her mother?_____

_____

_____

Underline details that tell how Juanita feels.

Reread

Author's Craft

How does the author help you understand what *frijoles* means?

FIND TEXT EVIDENCE

Read

Paragraphs 1–3

Point of View

How does Mamá feel about Juanita's decision?

_____

_____

Circle text evidence.

Paragraphs 4–6

Events

Underline three events that show this is a fairy tale.

Paragraph 6

Summarize

Why does the maid tell Juanita to hide? **Draw a box around the reason.**

Reread

Author's Craft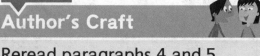

Reread paragraphs 4 and 5. How does the author help you visualize the beanstalk?

Juanita thought carefully as she **considered** the man's offer. He seemed caring and considerate. Certainly he would be kind to Pepe, so Juanita finally decided to sell Pepe. She accepted the beans.

When Juanita got home, Mamá was upset with her decision. "You have returned home with no food and no money!" she exclaimed.

Juanita had to **admit** that Mamá was right. All she had were three beans, and she still missed Pepe. Worst of all, Mamá was unhappy.

Juanita planted the beans in the backyard and went to bed. The next morning she woke up and went outside. A gigantic beanstalk as tall as the clouds stood where Juanita had planted the beans.

Juanita was curious. "I'm going to see what's up there," she said to herself, so Juanita climbed the beanstalk. At the top she saw a grand and **magnificent** palace in the middle of a field. She knocked on the door and a maid answered.

"Hide!" cried the maid. "The giant is coming now, and he doesn't like strangers." So Juanita quickly crawled under the table.

The giant stomped in carrying an unhappy hen in a cage. He said, "Lay, hen, lay!" Juanita's curiosity grew, and she peeked from under the table. Then she saw the hen's **creation**. Juanita gasped. It was a golden egg!

The poor hen reminded Juanita of Pepe. She wanted to give it a better home. She ran between the giant's legs and grabbed the cage. She raced to the beanstalk. The giant roared in anger and chased after her. Juanita was able to slide down the beanstalk, but the giant was too heavy. He caused the stalk to break and crash to the ground. The beanstalk was gone forever, and Juanita and the hen were safe.

The hen was happy to have a new home and laid many golden eggs. Mamá was happy to use the eggs to buy everything they needed. And Juanita was happy because she was able to trade a golden egg with the old man to get Pepe back!

Chris Vallo

Summarize

Use your notes and think about the sequence of events in "Juanita and the Beanstalk." Summarize the important events.

FIND TEXT EVIDENCE 🔍

> Read

Paragraphs 1–2
Summarize

Why does Juanita want the hen? **Underline** key details.

Paragraph 3
Point of View

How does Mamá feel about the hen?

_____

_____

Circle text evidence.

> Reread

Author's Craft

How does the author help you understand how Juanita feels at the end of the fairy tale?

Fluency

Take turns reading the first paragraph with expression. Talk about how the giant sounds.

Vocabulary

Use the sentences to talk with a partner about each word. Then answer the questions.

admit

María had to **admit** to her mom that she had broken the plate.

What is something you had to admit?

_____

_____

barter

Ashton likes to **barter**, or trade, toys with Kim.

What is another word for barter?

_____

_____

considered

Manuel thought carefully as he **considered** which apple to buy.

What is something you considered doing?

_____

_____

creation

Ella admired her **creation** in art class.

What is a creation you have made?

_____

_____

humble

My grandfather's house is **humble**, simple, and plain.

What is the opposite of humble?

_____

_____

Build Your Word List Reread the first paragraph on page 37. Draw a box around the word _gasped_. Look up the definition of the word _gasped_ using a dictionary. In your writer's notebook, make a list of words that mean almost the same as _gasped_. Use one of them in a sentence.

magnificent

Li took a picture of the **magnificent** sunset.

What is something magnificent you've seen?

_____

_____

payment

Mom gave our neighbor **payment** for the books.

What do people usually use for payment?

_____

_____

reluctantly

The goats stepped **reluctantly** down the steep path.

How would you raise your hand reluctantly?

_____

_____

Root Words

A root word is the simplest form of a word. When you read an unfamiliar word, look for the root word. Then use the root word to figure out what the word means.

🔍 FIND TEXT EVIDENCE

On page 36, I see the word considerate. *I think the root word is* consider. *I know that* consider *means "to think about it." Being* considerate *means "thoughtful of others' feelings."*

Juanita thought carefully as she considered the man's offer. He seemed caring and considerate.

Your Turn Find the root word in each word. Use it to figure out the word's meaning.

decision, page 36 _____

_____

curiosity, page 37 _____

_____

Summarize

When you summarize, you retell the most important events in a story. Use details to help you summarize "Juanita and the Beanstalk."

FIND TEXT EVIDENCE

Why does Juanita have to sell her pet goat? Identify important story events. Summarize them in your own words.

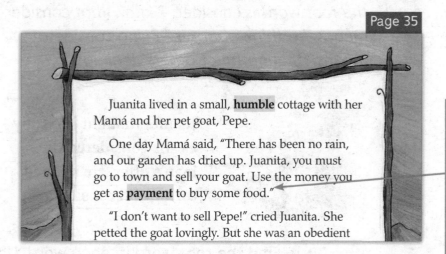

Page 35

Juanita lived in a small, **humble** cottage with her Mamá and her pet goat, Pepe.

One day Mamá said, "There has been no rain, and our garden has dried up. Juanita, you must go to town and sell your goat. Use the money you get as **payment** to buy some food."

"I don't want to sell Pepe!" cried Juanita. She petted the goat lovingly. But she was an obedient

I read that it hadn't rained and Mamá's garden dried up. They needed money for food. Mamá told Juanita to sell Pepe, her pet goat. These details help me summarize. Juanita had to sell her goat to get money for food.

Your Turn Reread "Juanita and the Beanstalk." Summarize the most important events in order that tell how Juanita found the giant's palace. Then write the answer here.

_____

_____

Events and Messages

"Juanita and the Beanstalk" is a fairy tale. A **fairy tale**

- Is a made-up story with events that could not happen
- Usually has magical characters or settings
- Almost always has a happy ending with a message

🔍 FIND TEXT EVIDENCE

I can tell that "Juanita and the Beanstalk" is a fairy tale. A huge beanstalk could not grow overnight in real life. There are also magical characters. The story has a happy ending, too.

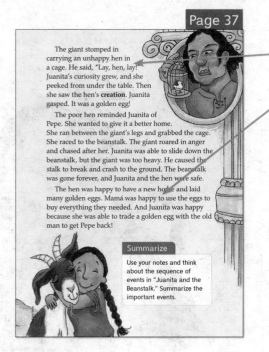

Page 37

The giant stomped in carrying an unhappy hen in a cage. He said, "Lay, hen, lay!" Juanita's curiosity grew, and she peeked from under the table. Then she saw the hen's **creation**. Juanita gasped. It was a golden egg!

The poor hen reminded Juanita of Pepe. She wanted to give it a better home. She ran between the giant's legs and grabbed the cage. She raced to the beanstalk. The giant roared in anger and chased after her. Juanita was able to slide down the beanstalk, but the giant was too heavy. He caused the stalk to break and crash to the ground. The beanstalk was gone forever, and Juanita and the hen were safe.

The hen was happy to have a new home and laid many golden eggs. Mamá was happy to use the eggs to buy everything they needed. And Juanita was happy because she was able to trade a golden egg with the old man to get Pepe back!

Summarize

Use your notes and think about the sequence of events in "Juanita and the Beanstalk." Summarize the important events.

Events

Important events in a fairy tale could not really happen.

Message

Fairy tales usually have a happy ending with a message.

Your Turn With a partner, find two details that show this is a fairy tale. How is this story like other fairy tales you know? Write your answer below.

_____

_____

_____

_____

Point of View

A character often has thoughts about other characters or events in a story. This is the point of view. Look for details to figure out the character's point of view. These details can help you learn more about the relationship between the main character and the minor, or other, characters.

Figuring out a character's point of view helps you understand his or her actions and relationship to other characters. If you don't understand why a character acts a certain way, reread and look for evidence of the character's point of view.

FIND TEXT EVIDENCE

Juanita is the main character. Pepe the goat is a minor character. What does Juanita think about Pepe? I can reread page 35 to see what Juanita says and does. These details will help me figure out Juanita's point of view about the goat.

Details
Juanita tells Mamá that she does not want to sell Pepe.
She pets the goat lovingly.

Point of View

Your Turn Reread "Juanita and the Beanstalk." Write details about Juanita's feelings for Pepe in the graphic organizer. Figure out her point of view. Do you agree with Juanita's point of view?

Chris Vallo

Details

↓

Juanita's Point of View

Respond to Reading

COLLABORATE

Talk about the prompt below. Think about Juanita's point of view.

How does the author show that Pepe is important to Juanita?

_____

_____

_____

_____

_____

_____

_____

_____

_____

_____

Plan a Business

Think about Sue and her lemonade stand on page 32. What did she need to do to create her business?

To create a business, you need a **plan**. First, decide what to sell. Next, make a list of the supplies you'll need. Then, think about how to advertise and how much you'll charge. The last thing to do is set a goal. Look back at page 32. Write a plan for Sue's stand.

What to sell: _____

Supplies: _____

How to advertise and what to charge: _____

Sue's goal: _____

Quick Tip

You need to charge more than you spend. List how much your supplies cost. Think how much people will be willing to pay. Then decide what to charge.

Make a Business Plan Think of a business you would like to start. Maybe you want to start a dog-walking service or make greeting cards to sell. Talk to adults to help you make a business plan.

What to sell: _____

Supplies: _____

How to advertise and what to charge: _____

My goal: _____

BUSINESS PLAN

What to sell: _Lemonade_

Supplies: _lemons, water, sugar, pitcher, glasses, stand_

How to advertise: _____

What to Charge: _____

Your goal: _____

Clever Jack Takes the Cake

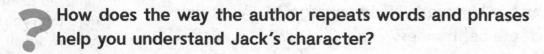

? **How does the way the author repeats words and phrases help you understand Jack's character?**

Literature Anthology: pages 390–407

Talk About It Reread the fifth paragraph on page 393. Talk with a partner about what Jack is doing.

Cite Text Evidence What words does the author repeat? Write text evidence and explain how it helps you understand what Jack is like.

 Make Inferences

Use text evidence and what you know to make an inference. An inference is like an educated guess. What inference can you make about how much time Jack is spending in the strawberry patch?

Text Evidence	Jack

Write The author uses repetition to help me understand that Jack is

_____

_____

How does the author use language to help you visualize what the bear is doing?

Talk About It Reread page 401. Talk with your partner about what the bear does.

Cite Text Evidence What words and phrases help you visualize what happens to Jack's cake? Write text evidence in the chart.

Text Evidence	What I Visualize

Write The author uses words and phrases to help me visualize _____

_____

_____

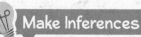

? **How does the illustration help you understand Jack's story?**

Talk About It Reread page 404 and look at the illustration. Talk with a partner about the parts of Jack's story.

Cite Text Evidence What clues in the illustration help you understand what Jack tells the princess? Write clues in the chart.

Illustration Clue	How It Helps

Write The author uses the illustration to help me see that Jack

_____

_____

Quick Tip

When I reread, I can use illustrations to help myself understand more about the story.

 Evaluate Information

Jack gulps and shuffles his feet before greeting the princess. What does this say about how Jack is feeling?

Respond to Reading

COLLABORATE

Answer the prompt below. Think about how the author helps you visualize the events in the story. Use your notes and graphic organizer.

How does the author use text and illustrations to show how Jack accomplishes his goal?

_____

_____

_____

_____

_____

_____

_____

_____

_____

_____

Quick Tip

Use these sentence starters to organize your text evidence.

The author describes how Jack . . .

The illustrations help me see . . .

This helps me know that Jack . . .

Self-Selected Reading

Choose a text. In your writer's notebook, write the title, author, and genre of the book. As you read, make a connection to ideas in other texts you have read or to a personal experience. Write your ideas in your notebook.

Money — Then and Now

Literature Anthology:
pages 410–413

Earn and Spend

1   People earn money by working hard. They might have a job or invent something new. They might even start their own business. You might not be old enough to have a job, but there are many ways you can earn money. Lots of kids help their neighbors by raking leaves or walking dogs to earn cash. Some parents even give their kids an allowance in exchange for helping around the house.

2   What do you do with the money you earn? Well, you have a few choices. The easiest one is to spend the money you make on things you want or need. Spending money is easy. Learning to save money can be challenging.

Reread and use the prompts to take notes in the text.

In paragraph 1, **circle** the word *exchange*. **Underline** context clues that help you find the meaning of the word. Write the meaning here:

_____

_____

_____

Reread paragraph 2. **Draw a box around** the two different ways you can use money.

COLLABORATE

Talk with a partner about how the ways you can use money are different. **Make marks** beside text evidence that describes how they are different.

Skip ODonnell/E+/Getty Images

Save and Donate

3   Saving money is important so that when you need it, you will have it. Many people put the money they want to save into a savings account at the bank. Then the bank pays interest, or money for every month the money stays at the bank.

4   Some people save some of their money, but want to help others, too. Donating money means giving it to someone who needs it to do something good. Maybe you want to help groups who work with dogs and cats. Maybe you want to help people clean up the oceans. Making a donation helps pay for the things these people do.

In paragraph 3, **circle** the word *interest*. **Underline** context clues that can help you figure out the meaning of the word. Write the meaning here:

_____

_____

_____

COLLABORATE

Reread paragraph 4. **Draw boxes** around different groups you could donate money to. Talk with a partner about how your donations would help others. **Make a mark** beside the statement that shows how.

Donate   Save   Spend

How does the author help you understand what she thinks about saving and donating money?

 Talk About It Reread the excerpt on page 51. Talk with a partner about what the author thinks about saving and donating money. This will help you figure out the author's point of view.

Cite Text Evidence How do you know what the author thinks about saving and donating money? Write text evidence in the chart.

Details

Point of View

Write I know what the author thinks about saving and donating

money because _____

_____

_____

_____

Voice

A writer's use of language can express a personality or voice. For example, perfect grammar and serious sounding words create a formal voice. Language you might use while talking to a friend creates an informal voice.

FIND TEXT EVIDENCE

In paragraph 1 of the excerpt on page 51, the author writes "Saving money is important so that when you need it, you will have it." Here, perfect grammar and a serious tone create a formal voice.

> Saving money is important so that when you need it, you will have it. Many people put the money they want to save into a savings account at the bank.

Your Turn Reread paragraph 2 on page 51.

- How do you know the author is using a formal voice? _____

_____

_____

Text Connections

? **How do the poet of "Here's a Nut" and the author of** *Clever Jack Takes the Cake* **help you visualize how the characters meet their needs?**

COLLABORATE

Talk About It Read the poem. Talk with a partner about how the squirrels in the poem get what they need.

Cite Text Evidence **Circle** clues in the poem that show that there are plenty of nuts. **Underline** how the squirrels get what they need.

Write I can visualize how Jack and the squirrels in the poem get what they need because _____

_____

_____

_____

_____

_____

_____

Ingram Publishing/SuperStock

Quick Tip

In the poem, the squirrels find a way to get what they need. This will help me compare the poem with a story I read this week.

Here's a Nut

Here's a nut, there's a nut;
Hide it quick away,
In a hole, under leaves,
To eat some winter day.
Acorns sweet are plenty,
We will have them all:
Skip and scamper lively
Till the last ones fall.

— Louisa May Alcott

Present Your Work

Decide how you will present your business plan to the class. Create an online slideshow or a digital poster. Bring samples. Use the checklist to help yourself improve your presentation.

Before I present, I will organize my presentation by

_____

_____

Organizing a presentation is important because _____

_____

Quick Tip

Note cards are an excellent way to organize a presentation. Use note cards to record information about each idea and to help yourself remember key ideas.

✔ Presenting Checklist

- ☐ I will organize my presentation using note cards.
- ☐ I will support most ideas with at least three points.
- ☐ I will practice my presentation.
- ☐ I will be sure my sample product is fun to share.

Essential Question

What are different kinds of energy?

Carlos lives near a wind farm. Wind power makes electricity that heats his house. Energy comes from different sources. Energy from the wind and the Sun is renewable. That means it will never run out. Look at the photograph. Talk about the kinds of energy you see. Write what you see and know about energy in the word web.

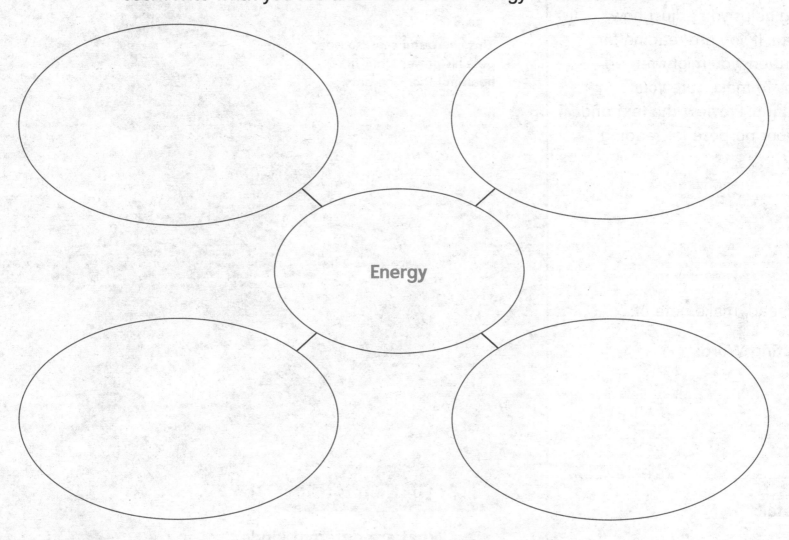

Energy

Go online to **my.mheducation.com** and read the "Can You Hear Me?" Blast. Think about different kinds of energy. Then blast back your response.

TIME FOR KIDS·

TAKE NOTES

Understanding why you are reading helps you adjust how you read. If you are reading for information, you might reread sections to make sure you understand. Preview the text and write your purpose for reading.

_____

_____

_____

As you read, make note of:

Interesting Words: _____

_____

_____

_____

Key Details: _____

_____

_____

_____

This energetic snowboarder gets his power from the healthful foods he eats.

© Corey Rich/Aurora Open/Corbis

Essential Question

? **What are different kinds of energy?**

Read why solar energy is a good source of power.

Here Comes Solar Power

What do you have in common with a car and a factory? You both need **energy** to run. Energy keeps things moving.

Energy Today

You get your energy because you eat healthful foods. Most factories, homes, and cars get their energy from fossil fuels. Coal, petroleum, and natural gas are fossil fuels. They have been the **traditional,** or usual, energy **sources** for more than a century. Today, most of the energy we use in the United States comes from burning fossil fuels.

But these fuels come from deep under Earth's surface, and they are running out. They cannot be reused. Once a fossil fuel is gone, it's gone forever. So we need alternative energy sources to **replace** them. Scientists are looking for new, alternative sources of energy that won't run out. Solar power is one good alternative to fossil fuels.

ARGUMENTATIVE TEXT

FIND TEXT EVIDENCE

Read

Paragraphs 1-2

Cause and Effect

Underline what happens when you eat healthful foods. What signal word helps you know this?

_____

Paragraph 3

Ask and Answer Questions

What happens when a fossil fuel is gone?

_____

_____

Circle text evidence. Write your own question about fossil fuels.

_____

_____

Reread

Author's Craft

How does the author get you excited about solar power?

FIND TEXT EVIDENCE

Read

Paragraphs 1–2

Headings

What claim does the heading make about solar power?

Underline three key ideas that support this claim.

Paragraphs 1–2

Homophones

Draw a box around a word that sounds the same as *two*.

Write another one here. _____

Sidebar

Cause and Effect

What causes electricity to flow into buildings? **Circle** the cause.

Reread

Author's Craft

Why is "Solar Power Deserves Its Day in the Sun" a good heading for this section?

Solar Power Deserves Its Day in the Sun

Solar power is one source of **renewable** energy. And it is not expensive. Solar panels are getting cheaper to build and install every year. And sunlight is free, too! When people get energy from fossil fuels, they have to pay for all of the coal, oil, and natural gas that is burned up.

Solar power is also better for the environment because it doesn't produce **pollution**. The pollution caused by fossil fuels can harm the quality of the air that we all need to breathe.

Solar panels are placed on the roof of a building.

How Solar Panels Work

Solar power is natural. That means it isn't made or changed by people. On a bright day, the sun's rays hit solar panels and cause them to produce electricity. The electricity then flows into buildings. As a result, there is enough energy to cool or heat homes, and to power lights, stoves, and computers.

COUNTERPOINT · POINT

What Happens on a Rainy Day?

There are some drawbacks to solar energy. For one, if the Sun isn't shining, energy can't be produced. If it's nighttime or too cloudy, solar panels won't create any electricity. Scientists are designing more efficient batteries. These can charge up while the Sun is shining so that people can use solar power even after the Sun goes down. But those batteries can still run out if a lot of power is being used.

A Bright Future

Millions of people around the world use solar power to produce electricity for their homes and businesses. These people are finding that solar energy can do just about everything that fossil fuels do.

One day solar power might completely replace power from fossil fuels. That's good news for the environment!

Summarize

Use your notes to summarize both claims in "Here Comes Solar Power."

(l) Holger Burmeister/Alamy Stock Photo; (bkgd) Evgeny Kuklev/Vetta/Getty Images; (r) Cultura Creative/Alamy

FIND TEXT EVIDENCE

Read

Paragraph 1
Ask and Answer Questions
What happens when the Sun isn't shining?

_____

_____

Circle text evidence.

Paragraphs 2–3
Cause and Effect
What is the effect of replacing fossil fuels?

_____

_____

Underline text evidence.

Reread
Author's Craft

How does the author help you understand what *drawbacks* are?

Vocabulary

Use the sentences to talk with a partner about each word. Then answer the questions.

energy

Good food gives Ron the **energy** he needs to play basketball with his friends.

Where do cars get their energy?

_____

_____

natural

Cotton is a **natural** material used to make clothes.

Name a natural material that is used in buildings.

_____

_____

Build Your Word List Find the word _designing_ on page 61. Write it in your writer's notebook. Use a word web to write more forms of the word. Use a dictionary to help.

pollution

Water **pollution**, such as garbage and chemicals, can harm animals.

Name something that causes air pollution.

_____

_____

produce

Solar panels can **produce** enough electricity to heat a whole house.

What word means the same as _produce?_

_____

_____

renewable

Trees are a **renewable** resource because more will always grow.

What does the word _renewable_ mean?

_____

_____

replace

Soon Tina will **replace** her car with one that runs on electricity.

Name something that you can replace.

_____

_____

sources

Wind and solar power are two **sources** of energy we can use.

What are your energy sources?

_____

_____

traditional

Staying up late is a **traditional** way to celebrate New Year's.

What is another word for _traditional?_

_____

_____

Homophones

Homophones are words that sound the same but have different meanings and spellings. The words _sea_ and _see_ are homophones. Use context clues to figure out a homophone's meaning.

FIND TEXT EVIDENCE

I see the word need _on page 59._ Need _and_ knead _are homophones._ Need _means "to require something."_ Knead _means "to mix with your hands." I can use context clues to figure out what_ need _means. Here it means "to require."_

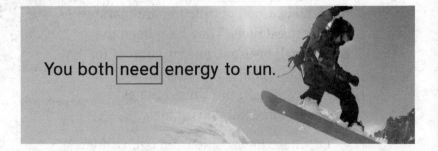

You both need energy to run.

Your Turn Use context clues to figure out what this word means. Then find its homophone.

rays, page 60 _____

_____

_____

Ask and Answer Questions

Asking yourself questions as you read helps you better understand what you are reading. Ask yourself questions as you read "Here Comes Solar Power." Then, look for details to support your answers.

🔍 FIND TEXT EVIDENCE

Look at the section "Energy Today" on page 59. Think of a question. Then reread to answer it.

> Page 59
>
> You get your energy because you eat healthful foods. Most factories, homes, and cars get their energy from fossil fuels. Coal, petroleum, and natural gas are fossil fuels. They have been the **traditional,** or usual, energy **sources** for more than a century. Today, most of the energy we use in the United States comes from burning fossil fuels.
>
> But these fuels come from deep under Earth's surface, and they are running out. They cannot be reused. Once a fossil fuel is gone, it's gone forever. So we need alternative energy

I have a question. What are fossil fuels? I read that most factories, homes, and cars run on fossil fuels. They come from deep under Earth's surface and are running out. Now I can answer my question. Fossil fuels come from the Earth and will not always be here.

Your Turn Reread page 60. Think of a question about solar energy. Write it here. Talk with a partner about the answer.

_____

_____

Headings and Sidebars

"Here Comes Solar Power" is an **argumentative text**. Argumentative texts

- state an opinion and persuade readers to agree with it
- support claims, or statements that something is true, with evidence
- include text features such as headings and sidebars

FIND TEXT EVIDENCE

I can tell that "Here Comes Solar Power" is an argumentative text. It states the opinion that solar power is a useful energy source. It makes claims supported by facts. It has headings that tell about each section. It also has a sidebar.

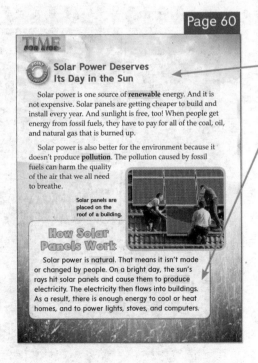

Page 60

TIME FOR KIDS

Solar Power Deserves Its Day in the Sun

Solar power is one source of **renewable** energy. And it is not expensive. Solar panels are getting cheaper to build and install every year. And sunlight is free, too! When people get energy from fossil fuels, they have to pay for all of the coal, oil, and natural gas that is burned up.

Solar power is also better for the environment because it doesn't produce **pollution**. The pollution caused by fossil fuels can harm the quality of the air that we all need to breathe.

Solar panels are placed on the roof of a building.

How Solar Panels Work

Solar power is natural. That means it isn't made or changed by people. On a bright day, the sun's rays hit solar panels and cause them to produce electricity. The electricity then flows into buildings. As a result, there is enough energy to cool or heat homes, and to power lights, stoves, and computers.

Readers to Writers

A claim is a statement that something is true. In an argumentative text, the writer tries to convince you that his or her claim is true. When you write an argumentative text, use facts and evidence to support your claims.

Headings

Headings suggest what a section of text is mainly about.

Sidebar

A sidebar gives extra information about a topic.

Your Turn Reread the sidebar on page 60. Talk about how solar panels work. Write one detail here.

COLLABORATE

_____

_____

Cause and Effect

A cause is why something happens. An effect is what happens. They happen in time order. Signal words such as *so, as a result,* and *because* help you find causes and effects.

🔍 FIND TEXT EVIDENCE

On page 59, I read that we need to replace fossil fuels with alternative energy sources. This is the effect. I can find the cause. Once a fossil fuel is gone, it's gone forever. I can connect this cause and effect with the word so. Fossil fuels run out, so we need alternative energy sources.

Quick Tip

Signal words can help you find causes and effects, but they're not always present. Looking for a relationship between two facts that seem closely linked can also help. Ask yourself: *Did one of these things make the other one happen?*

Cause	➡	Effect
Once a fossil fuel is gone, it's gone forever.	➡	We need to replace fossil fuels with alternative energy sources.

Your Turn Reread "Here Comes Solar Power." Use signal words to find more causes and effects. Write them in the graphic organizer.

Holger Burmeister/Alamy Stock Photo

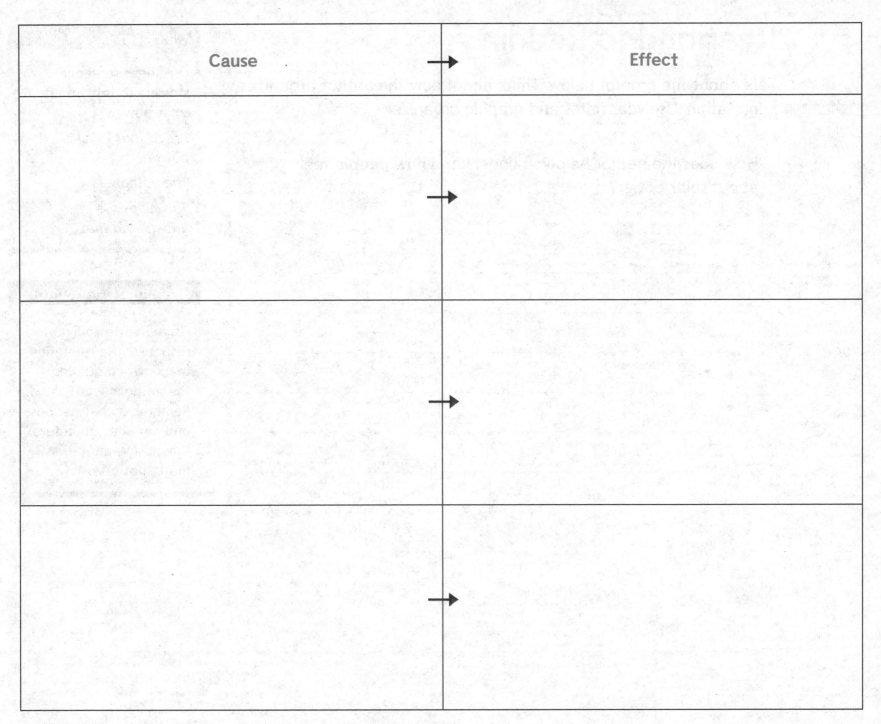

Cause	→	Effect
	→	
	→	
	→	

Respond to Reading

COLLABORATE

Talk about the prompt below. Think about how the author organizes information. Use your notes and graphic organizer.

How does the author help you understand how people feel about solar power?

_____

_____

_____

_____

_____

_____

_____

_____

_____

_____

Quick Tip

Use these sentence starters to talk about solar power.

I read that solar power . . .

The author . . .

This helps me understand that . . .

Grammar Connections

As you write your response, use quotation marks when quoting the author's words. Remember that periods and commas go before the closing quotation mark, not after it.

Asking Questions

Generating, or asking, questions is a good way to learn more about a topic. Questions can help you figure out how things are alike and different. Placing answers in a chart helps you compare information.

	Is it renewable?	Does it pollute?
Natural Gas	No	Yes
Hydropower	Yes	No

Look at the chart. What two energy sources does it compare?

Which energy source is renewable?

Make a Chart Research two energy sources to compare. Use the sample chart and these steps to make your own chart.

1. Draw a chart.
2. Write the energy sources in the first column. Write your questions in the first row.
3. Answer the questions by filling in the chart.

Danita Delimont/Alamy Stock Photo

It's All in the Wind

Literature Anthology: pages 414–417

? How does the author help you understand what the wind can do for people?

COLLABORATE

Talk About It Reread page 415. Turn to a partner and talk about what the wind can do.

Cite Text Evidence What words describe how people have used the wind? Write text evidence in the chart.

Text Evidence	What I Understand

Write I understand how the wind helps people because the author

_____

_____

_____

Evaluate Information

The author claims that "People have been using wind as an energy source since ancient times." What evidence does the author use to support this claim? Is the evidence convincing?

How does the author use text features to help you understand how wind turbines can power a town?

Talk About It Look at the diagram and photograph on page 416. Talk with a partner about what these text features show.

Cite Text Evidence How do these text features help you understand how wind turbines provide electricity? Write how in the chart.

Text Feature	Clue	How It Helps

Write The text features help me understand how wind turbines can power a town by _____

_____

_____

Quick Tip

When I reread, I can think about how each text feature helps me understand the topic better.

Make Inferences

An inference is a guess based on evidence. Use the photograph to make an inference about why some people don't want wind farms in their towns.

Respond to Reading

COLLABORATE

Answer the prompt below. Think about the reasons the author gives to support wind energy. Use your notes and graphic organizer.

How does the author help you understand why some people claim wind energy is useful while other people claim it isn't?

_____

_____

_____

_____

_____

_____

_____

_____

_____

_____

Self-Selected Reading

Choose a text. In your writer's notebook, write the title, author, and genre of the book. As you read, make a connection to ideas in other texts you have read or to a personal experience. Write your ideas in your notebook.

Power for All

Literature Anthology:
pages 418–419

1.   Every day, students in many countries are in a race against the Sun. Many don't have electricity. For this reason, they must do their homework during the daylight hours or use dangerous oil lamps or candlelight at night.

2.   In Tsumkwe (CHOOM-kwee), a small town in Namibia, Africa, villagers were lucky. Until recently, they got all their electricity from a generator powered by oil. However, there were problems with the generator. It cost a lot of money. And it only produced electricity for three hours each day.

Reread and use the prompts to take notes in the text.

In paragraph 1, **underline** text evidence that explains why students must race against the Sun. Write it here:

_____

_____

_____

Circle the words in paragraph 2 that help you understand where Tsumkwe is located.

COLLABORATE

Reread paragraph 2. Talk with a partner about why the generator didn't solve the villagers' problems. **Make marks** in the margin next to text evidence that supports your discussion.

? **How does the author's word choice help you visualize life without electricity?**

COLLABORATE

Talk About It Reread the excerpt on page 73. Turn and talk with a partner about what life was like in Tsumkwe, Namibia.

Cite Text Evidence What words and phrases help you visualize what life would be like without electricity? Write text evidence in the chart.

Text Evidence	What I Visualize

Write The author helps me visualize what life would be like without

electricity by _____

_____

Quick Tip

When I reread, I can visualize, or create pictures in my mind, by paying attention to interesting details.

Make Inferences

An inference is a guess based on evidence. Use text evidence and what you know to make an inference about why oil lamps and candles might be dangerous light sources.

Text Features

Writers use print and graphic features such as sidebars and maps to help readers better understand a topic. Sometimes they use print and graphic features to explain their point of view.

🔍 FIND TEXT EVIDENCE

On page 419 of "Power for All" in the **Literature Anthology,** *the author includes a sidebar with ideas about how to save energy. By saying that the five ways are easy, the author is sending a message that she thinks saving energy is something everyone can do.*

> Here are five easy ways that you can save energy every day. Try them all!

Your Turn Reread the sidebar on page 419.

- How do you know which energy saving tip is most important to the author? _____

  _____

- How do you know how the author feels about saving energy?

  _____

  _____

Davydenko Yuliia/Shutterstock.com

Readers to Writers

When you write, think about using sidebars, photographs, captions, graphs, lists, headings, or maps to help your readers understand the topic better. If you want to share your opinion, these text and graphic features can help you convince readers to agree with you.

Text Connections

? How do graphic features such as the painting below and the photographs and illustrations in "It's All in the Wind" and "Power for All" help you understand different kinds of energy?

Talk About It Look at the painting and read the caption. With a partner, discuss how the ship is moving.

Cite Text Evidence **Circle** clues in the painting that show what makes the ship move. **Underline** a detail that suggests the ship is moving.

Write The graphic features help me understand different types of energy

because _____

_____

_____

_____

_____

_____

This oil painting of an American schooner was painted sometime during the 19th century by an unknown artist.

Courtesy National Gallery of Art, Washington

Accuracy and Rate

Reading with accuracy means saying each word correctly and not leaving out any words or sentences. Use your knowledge of sounds and spellings to pronounce unfamiliar words. Reading with accuracy and at the appropriate rate makes a text's meaning clear and helps listeners understand it.

Page 418

In Tsumkwe (CHOOM-kwee), a small town in Namibia, Africa, villagers were lucky. Until recently, they got all their electricity from a generator powered by oil. However, there were problems with the generator. It cost a lot of money. And it only produced electricity for three hours each day.

The word Tsumkwe *is unfamiliar. I can use the information in parentheses to sound out the word before reading aloud. This will improve my accuracy.*

Quick Tip

If you have trouble pronouncing a new word, check the pronunciation in a dictionary.

Tech Tip

You can use an online dictionary to listen to the pronunciation of unfamiliar words.

Your Turn Turn to page 419 of the **Literature Anthology**. Take turns reading all four paragraphs aloud with a partner. Then think about how you did. Complete these sentences.

I remembered to _____

_____

Next time I will _____

_____

*Literature Anthology:
pages 414–417*

Expert Model

Features of an Opinion Essay

An **opinion essay** is a kind of argumentative text. An opinion essay

- clearly states the writer's claim, or opinion, about a topic
- supports the claim with convincing reasons and facts
- has a strong opening that makes the reader want to read on

Analyze an Expert Model Reread the section "A Breath of Fresh Air" on page 417 of "It's All in the Wind" in the **Literature Anthology**. Use text evidence to answer the questions.

How does the author help you understand one claim about wind energy?

_____

_____

Why is "A Breath of Fresh Air" a good heading for this section?

_____

_____

_____

Word Wise

Authors use linking words or phrases such as *also, in addition,* or *however* to connect ideas. For example, on page 416 the author says, "Some people also worry about the costs of wind energy." The linking word *also* is used to help you see that there are more reasons why people are not in favor of wind energy.

Plan: Choose Your Topic

COLLABORATE

Brainstorm With a partner, brainstorm a list of energy sources that would be good for you or your community. Use your notes on "It's All in the Wind" in your discussion. Use these sentence starters.

A good source of energy is . . .

This source would help by . . .

I know this because I read . . .

Writing Prompt Choose one energy source from your list. Write an opinion essay about it.

I will write about _____

Purpose and Audience Your purpose is your main reason for writing. Your audience is who will be reading what you write.

The purpose of my opinion essay is _____

_____

_____

_____

Plan In your writer's notebook, draw a Problem and Solution chart. Fill in the chart with two problems your energy source will solve.

Problem	Solution

Quick Tip

The purpose of your opinion essay is to state your opinion and convince others to agree with you. To do that, you will need to tell readers the reasons you are right. Research the topic to find facts to support your claim, or opinion.

Plan: Organization

Organization Opinion essays can be organized in many different ways. One way is to state a problem and make a claim about which solution you believe is needed. Then, present facts to support your claim.

Let's look at an expert model. Read this passage from "Here Comes Solar Power."

> Once fossil fuels are gone, they're gone forever. So we need alternative energy sources to replace them. Scientists are looking for new, alternative sources of energy that won't run out. Solar power is one good alternative to fossil fuels.

Underline the problem. How does the author help you understand what the solution is?

_____

_____

 Take Notes Research your energy source. Look for facts you can use to fill in the solutions boxes in your Problem and Solution chart.

Draft

Fact and Opinion An effective opinion essay lists reasons that support the writer's opinion. The most effective reasons are usually facts. Facts are statements that have been proven true. Opinions are statements based on feelings.

Read each sentence below. Then write whether it is a fact or an opinion on the line.

We should rely less on fossil fuels.

_____

Wind power can be cheaper than traditional fuel.

_____

Solar power is one alternative to fossil fuels.

_____

 Write a Draft Use your Problem and Solution chart to write a draft in your writer's notebook. Start with your opinion. Then use convincing facts to support it.

Imagemore/Glow Images

Revise

Strong Openings Use a strong opening to introduce your topic. One way is to use questions or fascinating facts to grab the reader's attention. A strong opening states the topic in a way that makes the reader want to keep reading.

Reread the opening paragraph of "Power for All." Then use text evidence to answer the question.

> Every day, students in many countries are in a race against the Sun. Many don't have electricity. For this reason, they must do their homework during daylight hours or use dangerous oil lamps or candlelight at night.

How does the author make you want to keep reading?

_____

_____

 Revise Use a strong opening. Think about adding, deleting, or combining details to improve sentence structure.

Ingram Publishing/SuperStock

Peer Conferences

Review a Draft Listen carefully as a partner reads his or her draft aloud. Tell your partner what you like about the draft. Use these sentence starters to talk about it.

I think your opening is . . .

Add another fact here to . . .

You did/did not convince me because . . .

I have a question about . . .

Partner Feedback After you finish giving each other feedback, write one suggestion your partner made that you will use in your revision.

_____

_____

_____

Revision After you finish your peer conference, use the Revising Checklist to figure out what you can change to make your opinion essay better. Remember to use the rubric on page 85 to help with your revision.

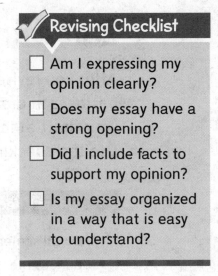

Revising Checklist

☐ Am I expressing my opinion clearly?

☐ Does my essay have a strong opening?

☐ Did I include facts to support my opinion?

☐ Is my essay organized in a way that is easy to understand?

Edit and Proofread

After you revise your opinion essay, edit and proofread it to find any mistakes in grammar, spelling, capitalization, and punctuation. Read your draft at least three times. This will help you catch any mistakes. Use the checklist below to edit your sentences.

Tech Tip

If you typed your draft on a computer, print it out. It is easier to find any mistakes you made on a printed copy than on the computer screen.

✔ Editing Checklist

☐ Do all sentences start with a capital letter and end with a punctuation mark?

☐ Are there linking words to connect ideas?

☐ Are apostrophes used correctly in contractions?

☐ Are all words spelled correctly?

Grammar Connections

When you proofread your draft for punctuation mistakes, remember that you should always use an apostrophe when writing contractions of pronouns and verbs such as *I'm* and *they're*.

List two mistakes that you found as you proofread your essay.

1 _____

_____

_____

2 _____

_____

_____

Publish, Present, and Evaluate

Publishing When you publish your writing, you create a neat final copy that is free of mistakes. As you write, be sure your cursive is legible. Check that you are holding your pencil between your thumb and forefinger.

Presentation When you are ready to present, practice your presentation. Use the presenting checklist.

Evaluate After you publish your essay, use the rubric to evaluate it.

✓ Presenting Checklist

- ☐ Look at your audience.
- ☐ Present your opinion clearly.
- ☐ Present your supporting facts in a convincing way.
- ☐ Answer questions thoughtfully.

What did you do well? _____

_____

What might need more work? _____

_____

4	3	2	1
• opinion is clearly stated in an exciting way • includes many supporting facts • several linking words are used and spelled correctly	• opinion is clearly stated • includes several supporting facts • linking words are used and spelled correctly	• opinion is somewhat unclear • includes a few supporting facts • one or two linking words are used but might be misspelled	• opinion is not stated • includes at least one supporting fact • linking words are not used • many spelling mistakes

Spiral Review

You have learned new skills and strategies in Unit 5 that will help you read more critically. Now it is time to practice what you have learned.

- **Ask and Answer Questions**
- **Author's Point of View**
- **Point of View**
- **Timeline**
- **Root Words**
- **Homophones**
- **Summarize**
- **Cause and Effect**

Connect to Content

- **Write a Blog Post**
- **Make a List**
- **Reading Digitally**

Read the selection and choose the best answer to each question.

RUBY BRIDGES:
Child of Change

[1]   When Ruby Bridges was six, her mother said, "Ruby you are going to a new school today, and you better behave." Ruby wasn't just any first grader going to any new school. She was making history.

[2]   Ruby Bridges was born on September 8, 1954, in Tylertown, Mississippi. When she was four years old, her family moved to New Orleans, Louisiana.

[3]   Remarkably, something else happened in 1954. At the time, there were many schools that African American students were not allowed to attend. On May 17, 1954, the U.S. Supreme Court ruled against this segregation of schools. The judges said schools should be integrated. Louisiana schools resisted the change.

[4]   When Ruby started kindergarten in 1959, she attended an all-African American school. But in 1960, the courts insisted Louisiana schools follow the law and integrate students. Ruby was given a test that determined which African American students would be allowed to attend the schools. She passed the test.

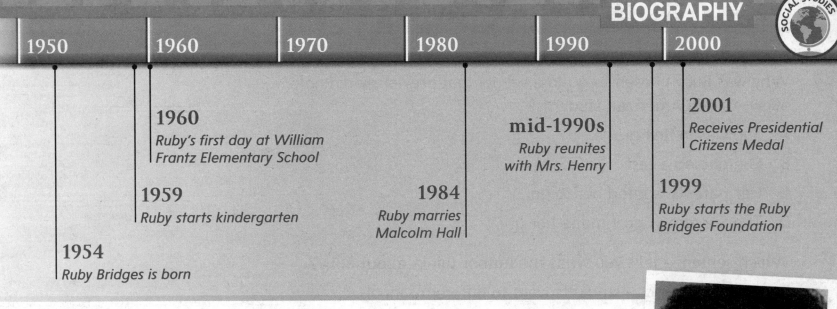

1950   1960   1970   1980   1990   2000

2001
Receives Presidential Citizens Medal

mid-1990s
Ruby reunites with Mrs. Henry

1960
Ruby's first day at William Frantz Elementary School

1999
Ruby starts the Ruby Bridges Foundation

1959
Ruby starts kindergarten

1984
Ruby marries Malcolm Hall

1954
Ruby Bridges is born

[5]   November 14, 1960, was Ruby's first day at the new school. The little girl held her head high as four U.S. marshals walked her into William Frantz Elementary School. The marshals protected her from angry people who lined the streets and stood outside the school. Some said horrible things to Ruby.

[6]   Ruby spent that first day in the principal's office because of the uproar. Many parents took their children out of school. For the rest of the year, Ruby was in a classroom by herself. Mrs. Henry was the only teacher willing to work with Ruby.

[7]   By second grade a lot changed. More and more students returned to the school. In time, other African American students attended as well. Years later,

Ruby graduated from a desegregated high school. She studied travel and became a travel agent. In 1984 she married Malcolm Hall, and they had four sons.

[8]   In the mid-1990s Ruby reunited with Mrs. Henry. In 1999, Ruby started the Ruby Bridges Foundation to increase tolerance and help end racism. In 2001, President Bill Clinton awarded Ruby a Presidential Citizens Medal.

[9]   Ruby Bridges was a little girl who wanted to go to school. What she became was a civil rights heroine.

1 Why was Ruby chosen to go to a school that previously did not allow African American students?

A She was in first grade.

B She passed a test.

C Her parents wanted her to go.

D The Supreme Court made her go.

2 Which sentence tells you what the author thinks about Ruby?

F African American students went to different schools.

G November 14, 1960 was Ruby's first day at the new school.

H Years later, Ruby graduated from a desegregated high school.

J What she became was a civil rights heroine.

3 Which events happened two years apart?

A Ruby starts kindergarten/Ruby starts elementary school

B Ruby marries Malcolm Hall/Ruby reunites with Mrs. Henry

C Ruby reunites with Mrs. Henry/Ruby starts Foundation

D Ruby starts Foundation/Ruby gets Presidential Medal

> **Quick Tip**
>
> When trying to figure out an author's point of view, look for words that suggest how the author feels.

4 The root word <u>segregate</u> means "to separate." The word <u>desegregate</u> means

F separate again

G do away with separation

H not able to separate

J prepare to separate

Read the selection and choose the best answer to each question.

The Tale of Bunny's
BUSINESS

1.   Once upon a time there was a rabbit named Bunny who wanted to start a business. As she was munching on a leaf of kale, she got an idea. "Everyone loves kale," she thought. "I can sell kale chips! They are delicious and good for you, too."

2.   Bunny wrote down what she would need to do. "That's a lot of work," she thought. "I bet Sammy Squirrel, Chippy Chipmunk, and Gabby Groundhog will help me. Then we'll all make money."

3.   She gathered her friends and shared her idea. "Who wants to join the business?" Bunny asked. All three friends raised their paws high in the air.

4.   The next day, Bunny was planting kale seeds when she spotted Sammy Squirrel. "Hi, Sammy! Can you help plant?"

5.   "Not today," Sammy said.

6.   A few weeks later, Bunny was picking kale leaves when she saw Chippy. "Hi, Chippy! Can you help pick kale leaves?"

7.   "Not today," Chippy said.

8.   The next day, Bunny was baking kale leaves when Gabby Groundhog lumbered by.

9.   "Hi Gabby! Can you help me bake the kale leaves?"

10.   "Not today," Gabby said.

12   The next day, Bunny opened her kale chip business. Sammy, Chippy, and Gabby walked by her stand. "Are you here to help sell kale chips?" Bunny asked.

13   "Not today," the three friends said.

14   Customers quickly lined up to buy Bunny's kale chips. She sold out in less than an hour. As soon as the last bag sold, Sammy, Chippy, and Gabby walked by again.

15   "How much money did we make?" asked Chippy.

16   "Did I hear you right?" Bunny said. "How much did we make?"

17   "It's our business, right Bunny?" asked Sammy.

18   "Actually, no," Bunny smiled. "It is not our business. It is my business. I planted the kale, picked the kale, baked the kale, and sold the kale. The money is mine, and I'm going to make even more tomorrow!"

HOMEMADE KALE CHIPS $1 A BAG

1 Which event happens first in the story?

A Gabby doesn't help Bunny bake kale chips.

B Bunny writes what she needs to do for her kale chip business.

C Sammy won't help Bunny plant kale seeds.

D Chippy asks Bunny how much money they made.

2 How does Bunny feel about her friends at the end of the story?

F let down

G worried

H helpless

J sorry

3 Which is an example of homophones from the story?

A hi/high

B make/bake

C our/my

D Chippy/Chipmunk

> **Quick Tip**
>
> Remember that a cause is why something happens. An effect is something that happens as a result of the cause.

4 What causes Bunny to say she will keep all the money from the kale chip business?

F The chips sell out in less than hour.

G The kale chip business is her idea.

H She does all the work for the kale chip business.

J She doesn't want to share the money.

COMPARING GENRES

- Reread the biography "Irma Rangel, Texas Lawmaker" on pages 2–5 of this book and the argumentative text "It's All in the Wind" on pages 414–417 of the **Literature Anthology**.

- Use the Venn diagram below to show how the two genres are the same and different.

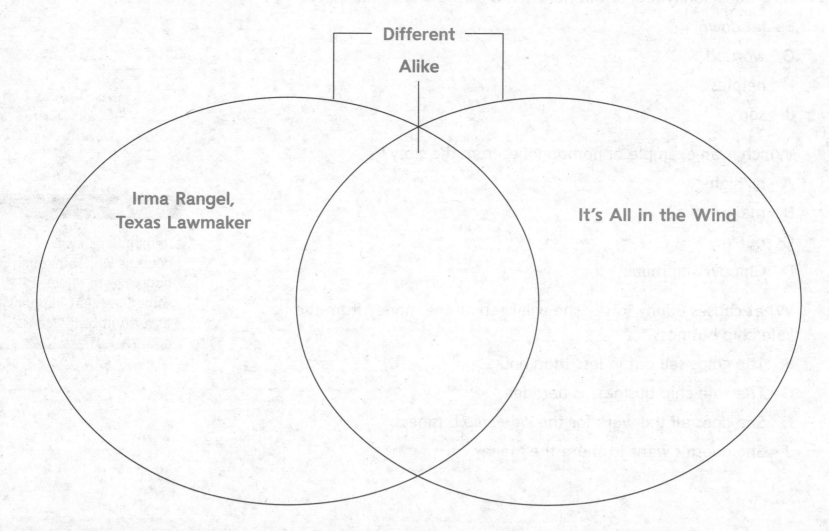

Different

Alike

Irma Rangel,
Texas Lawmaker

It's All in the Wind

HOMOPHONES AND HOMOGRAPHS

COLLABORATE

Homophones are words that sound the same but have different meanings and different spellings. The words *there* and *their* are homophones. Use context clues to figure out a homophone's meaning.

Circle the homophones in these sentences.

• Allen's team won the game by one point.

• Marco threw the ball through the hoop.

Homographs are words that are spelled the same but have different meanings. They are sometimes pronounced differently. You can check the meanings of homographs in a dictionary.

Underline the homographs in each sentence below. Then write what each homograph means.

• Kim can put her empty can in the recycling bin.

_____

_____

• They usually park the car across the street from the park.

_____

_____

WRITE A BLOG POST

The purpose of a blog post is to share information with others online. A blog post should include facts but can also include opinions.

- Make a list of first responders, such as firefighters. Write as many types of first responders as you can think of. Then choose one.

- Write questions for the first responder you chose. Use your questions to research first responders in your town.

- Write a blog post to teach others what you learned.

I decided to research _____

I want to ask _____

MAKE A LIST

Making a list can help you see all of the information you should know about a topic all at once.

- Choose one form of energy source and research it.

- Make a list of the positive and negative effects of using that energy source. Include only facts, not opinions.

I will research _____

A positive of using _____ is _____

RISING TO THE CHALLENGE

Log on to **my.mheducation.com** and read the online article "Rising to the Challenge," including the information found in the interactive elements. Answer the questions below.

Rising to the Challenge

After a natural disaster, young people worked together to save Japan.

Time for Kids: "Rising to the Challenge"

- Reread the section "An Earthquake Hits Japan." What is a tsunami?

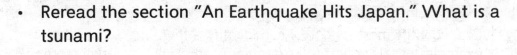

- In "Lining Up to Help," how does Kanazawa feel about volunteering to help other people?

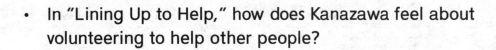

- Look at the map. Write the name of three cities closest to the epicenter of the earthquake.

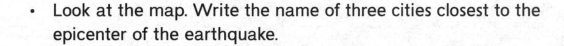

- Why is "Rising to the Challenge" a good title for this selection?

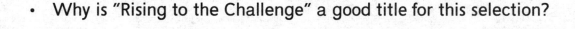

TRACK YOUR PROGRESS

WHAT DID YOU LEARN?

Use the rubric to evaluate yourself on the skills that you learned in this unit. Write your scores in the boxes below.

4	3	2	1
I can successfully identify all examples of this skill.	I can identify most examples of this skill.	I can identify a few examples of this skill.	I need to work on this skill more.

☐ Author's Point of View   ☐ Point of View   ☐ Cause and Effect

☐ Prefixes and Suffixes   ☐ Root Words   ☐ Homophones

Something I need to work more on is _____ because

_____

_____

_____

Text-to-Self Connecting a text to your own experiences helps you understand it better. Choose one text you read in this unit. Write a paragraph explaining a personal connection you made to it.

I made a personal connection to _____ because _____

_____

_____

Present Your Work

COLLABORATE

Discuss how you will present your energy source comparison chart to the class. Use the presenting checklist as you practice your presentation. Discuss the sentence starters below, and write your answers.

Quick Tip

Use a long pencil or straw to point to different parts of your chart as you present it. Avoid standing in front of your chart as you explain it.

	Is it renewable?	Does it pollute?
Natural Gas	No	Yes
Hydropower	Yes	No

An interesting fact I learned about sources of energy is

_____

_____

I would like to know more about _____

_____

Before I present, I will think about how to explain_____

_____

_____

I think my presentation was _____

_____

✓ Presenting Checklist

☐ I will practice presenting my chart.

☐ I will clearly name the two sources of energy I am comparing.

☐ I will explain the facts about each source of energy.

☐ Then I will point out how the two sources of energy compare.

Kayla had a goal. She wanted to win her race in the Special Olympics. Her goal was important to her, so she worked hard. Kayla is proud of herself today. Goals are important. They help us focus and learn new things. Achieving our goals makes us feel good about ourselves.

Look at the photograph. Talk about why goals are important. Write your ideas in the word web.

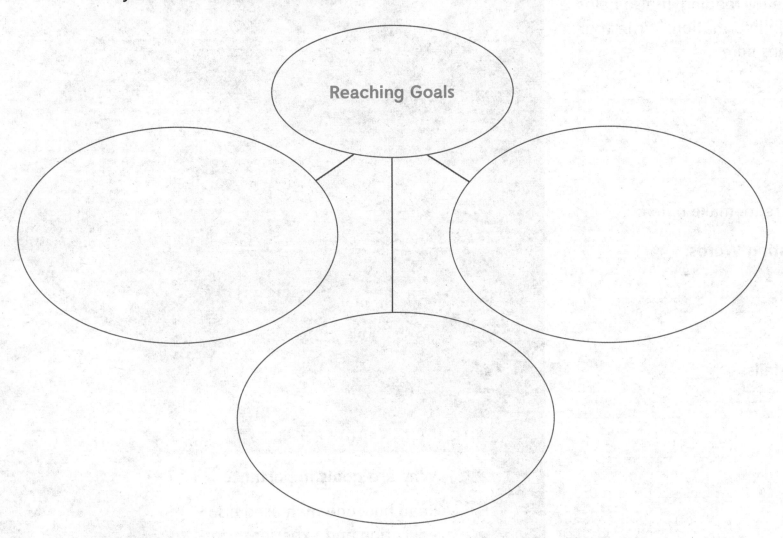

Reaching Goals

Go online to **my.mheducation.com** and read the "Mission: Juno" Blast. Think about why space exploration is important. Then blast back your response.

Vladimir Rys/Stringer/Getty Images Sport/Getty Images

TAKE NOTES

Asking questions before you read helps you figure out your purpose for reading. It also helps you gain information. Write your questions here.

_____

_____

_____

As you read, make note of:

Interesting Words: _____

_____

_____

Key Details: _____

_____

_____

_____

_____

_____

ROCKETING INTO SPACE

Essential Question

?

Why are goals important?

Read how one man used his education and experience to reach his goals.

When James A. Lovell Jr. was a boy, he loved to build rockets and launch them into the sky. But his dreams went a lot farther than his rockets. Like many boys who grew up in the 1930s, James dreamed of being a pilot. And as he watched his rockets soar, he knew someday he would, too.

HIGH FLYING DREAMS

James was born in Cleveland, Ohio, in 1928. He worked hard in school and planned to go to a special college to study **astronomy** and rockets. Unfortunately, he didn't have enough money to attend. James had to figure out another way to reach his **goal**.

James was **motivated** to find a way to fly rockets. So, he went to college near his home for two years and then signed up for flight training at the United States Naval Academy. After four years at the academy, James joined the United States Navy and became a **professional** naval test pilot. His job was to fly planes before anyone else was allowed to fly them.

NASA

James A. Lovell Jr. became an astronaut in 1962. He flew four space missions.

FIND TEXT EVIDENCE

Read

Paragraphs 1–2
Key Words
Find the key word and write it.

Underline details that show the keyword is important.

Paragraph 3
Reread
What did James do after he joined the Navy?

_____

_____

Circle text evidence to support your answer.

Reread
Author's Craft

How does the author help you understand how motivated James Lovell was to become an astronaut?

FIND TEXT EVIDENCE

Read

▼

Paragraph 1

Greek and Latin Roots

Circle the word *astronaut.* What does an astronaut do?

_____

_____

Paragraphs 2–4

Problem and Solution

What was the Apollo 13 crew's problem?

_____

_____

_____

Underline the first thing James did to solve it.

Photographs

Draw a box around how NASA's team is helping.

Reread

▼

Author's Craft

Why is "Big Challenges" a good heading for this section?

PILOT TO ASTRONAUT

As a pilot, James spent more than half of his flying time in jets. He taught other pilots how to fly. He also worked as a **specialist** in air flight safety. Soon, the National Aeronautics and Space Administration, or NASA, put out a call for astronauts. James applied for the job because he had all the **essential** skills needed to fly into space. As a result, NASA chose him. By 1962, James Lovell was an astronaut! He had finally reached his goal.

BIG CHALLENGES

James flew on three space missions, and then, in April 1970 he became commander of the Apollo 13 mission. This was a big responsibility and a great honor. This was also one of the biggest challenges of James's life.

Apollo 13 was supposed to land on the Moon. Two days after leaving Earth, however, the spacecraft had a **serious** problem. One of its oxygen tanks exploded. The crew did not have enough power or air to breathe. They could not make it to the Moon.

James **communicated** with the experts at NASA. No one knew what to do at first. Then the team on the ground did some **research** and came up with a solution. The astronauts followed the team's directions and built an invention using plastic bags, cardboard, and tape. It worked! It cleaned the air in the spacecraft. But the next problem was even bigger. How were the astronauts going to get back to Earth?

NASA's team works to solve Apollo 13's problem.

A JOB WELL DONE

The NASA team decided the astronauts would use the lunar, or moon, module as a lifeboat. James and the other two astronauts climbed into the smaller spacecraft and shut the hatch tight. They moved away from the main spaceship. With little power, water, food, or heat, the astronauts listened carefully to the team at NASA.

The trip back to Earth was dangerous and scary. For almost four days, the astronauts traveled in the cramped capsule. They were cold, thirsty, and hungry. Then, with millions of people watching on television, the module fell to Earth.

Years later, James Lovell said that Apollo 13 taught him how important it was for people to work together. His favorite memory was when the capsule splashed down in the Pacific Ocean and he knew they were safe.

A Dream Come True

DID YOU EVER DREAM OF GOING INTO SPACE? CHECK OUT SPACE CAMP!

Space camps have been around for more than 30 years. They make science, math, and technology exciting so kids will want to learn more. And like the NASA training programs, these camps teach the importance of teamwork and leadership.

The Apollo 13 crew splashed down safely on April 17, 1970.

(bkgd) NASA, (l) Bettmann/Getty

Summarize

Use your notes and think about the problems and solutions in "Rocketing into Space." Summarize the most important events in James Lovell's life.

BIOGRAPHY

FIND TEXT EVIDENCE

Read
Paragraphs 1–2
Reread

Why was the trip back to Earth so difficult?

_____

_____

_____

Circle text evidence.

Paragraphs 1–3
Problem and Solution
Underline the steps the astronauts took to solve the problem of getting back to Earth.

Reread
Author's Craft

How does the author help you understand how James Lovell felt about the Apollo 13 mission?

Vocabulary

Use the sentences to talk with a partner about each word. Then answer the questions.

communicated

Mora and her friends **communicated** by writing e-mails to each other.

What are some ways you have communicated with your friends?

_____

_____

essential

A toothbrush is an **essential** tool for cleaning teeth.

What is an essential tool you use in the classroom?

_____

_____

goal

Nick reached his **goal** and learned to swim.

Tell about a goal you have.

_____

_____

motivated

Jerry was **motivated** to learn to play her guitar, so she practiced every day.

What is something you are motivated to learn how to do?

_____

_____

professional

Ted works as a **professional** musician.

Name a professional athlete you know about.

_____

_____

Build Your Word List Reread the first paragraph on page 101. Draw a box around the word *soar*. In your writer's notebook, make a list of synonyms and antonyms for *soar*. Use a thesaurus to help you find more.

research

Melanie's mom is a scientist, and she uses a microscope to do **research**.

What animal would you like to research?

_____

_____

serious

Winnie pays attention because she is **serious** about getting good grades.

What is something you are serious about?

_____

_____

specialist

Dr. Morrison is a **specialist** in sports medicine.

What is something you know a lot about and could be a specialist in?

_____

_____

Greek and Latin Roots

Many words have word parts, such as Greek or Latin roots, in them. The Greek root *astro* means "star" and *naut* means "ship." The Latin root *luna* means "moon."

🔍 FIND TEXT EVIDENCE

On page 101, I see the word astronomy. I remember that astro *comes from a Greek word that means "star." I think astronomy may mean "the study of the stars."*

He worked hard in school and planned to go to a special college to study astronomy and rockets.

Your Turn Use the Greek or Latin root to figure out the meaning of the word.

lunar, page 103 _____

_____

_____

NASA

Reread

Stop and think about the text as you read. Are there new facts and ideas? Do they make sense? Reread to make sure you understand.

 FIND TEXT EVIDENCE

Reread "High Flying Dreams" on page 101. Do you understand what James A. Lovell Jr. did to become a pilot?

Quick Tip

Rereading helps you understand the text better. If you read something and you don't understand it, pause and reread. Look for details that help you understand the most important ideas.

Page 101

HIGH FLYING DREAMS

James was born in Cleveland, Ohio, in 1928. He worked hard in school and planned to go to a special college to study **astronomy** and rockets. Unfortunately, he didn't have enough money to attend. James had to figure out another way to reach his **goal**.

James was **motivated** to find a way to fly rockets. So, he went to college near his home for two years and then signed up for flight training at the United States Naval Academy. After four years at the academy, James joined the United States Navy and became a **professional** naval test pilot. His job was to fly planes before anyone else was allowed to fly them.

I read that James Lovell went to college and then to the United States Naval Academy. He signed up for flight training and became a professional naval test pilot. James Lovell became a pilot by going to school. He never gave up.

 Your Turn Reread pages 102 and 103. How did James Lovell get his Apollo 13 spaceship back home? Write the answer here.

Key Words and Photographs

"Rocketing into Space" is a **biography**. A biography

- tells the true story of a real person's life
- is written by another person
- includes text features such as key words, photographs, and captions

🔍 FIND TEXT EVIDENCE

I can tell that "Rocketing into Space" is a biography. It is the true story of James Lovell's life. It has photographs with captions and key words that are important to the biography.

Page 102

PILOT TO ASTRONAUT

As a pilot, James spent more than half of his flying time in jets. He taught other pilots how to fly. He also worked as a **specialist** in air flight safety. Soon, the National Aeronautics and Space Administration, or NASA, put out a call for astronauts. James applied for the job because he had all the **essential** skills needed to fly into space. As a result, NASA chose him. By 1962, James Lovell was an astronaut! He had finally reached his goal.

BIG CHALLENGES

James flew on three space missions, and then, in April 1970 he became commander of the Apollo 13 mission. This was a big responsibility and a great honor. This was also one of the biggest challenges of James's life.

Apollo 13 was supposed to land on the Moon. Two days

after leaving Earth, however, the spacecraft had a **serious** problem. One of its oxygen tanks exploded. The crew did not have enough power or air to breathe. They could not make it to the Moon.

James **communicated** with the experts at NASA. No one knew what to do at first. Then the team on the ground did some **research** and came up with a solution. The astronauts followed the team's directions and built an invention using plastic bags, cardboard, and tape. It worked! It cleaned the air in the spacecraft. But the next problem was even bigger. How were the astronauts going to get back to Earth?

NASA's team works to solve Apollo 13's problem.

Key Words
Key words are important words. They are in dark type.

Photographs
Photographs and their captions show more about the events in the person's life.

Readers to Writers

Look at the photograph and read the caption on page 102. What do they tell you about an important event in James Lovell's life?

When you write a biography, think about how you can use pictures and captions to tell more about the important events in the person's life.

Your Turn Find another key word. Why is this an important word in James Lovell's biography? Write your answer below.

_____

_____

Problem and Solution

Some informational texts have an organizational pattern such as problem and solution. The text describes a problem, tells the steps to solve the problem, and then gives the solution.

🔍 **FIND TEXT EVIDENCE**

James Lovell wanted to fly rockets but didn't have enough money to go to a special college. That was his problem. What steps did he take to solve his problem? What was the solution?

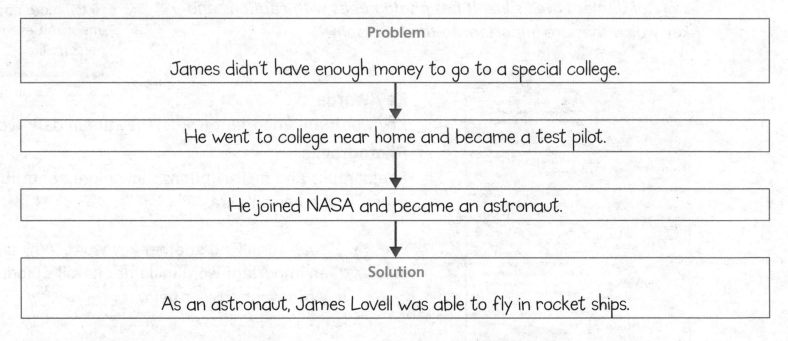

Problem
James didn't have enough money to go to a special college.

He went to college near home and became a test pilot.

He joined NASA and became an astronaut.

Solution
As an astronaut, James Lovell was able to fly in rocket ships.

Your Turn Reread "Big Challenges" on page 102. What was one of James's problems on Apollo 13? Find the steps he took to solve it and write them in your graphic organizer. Then write the solution.

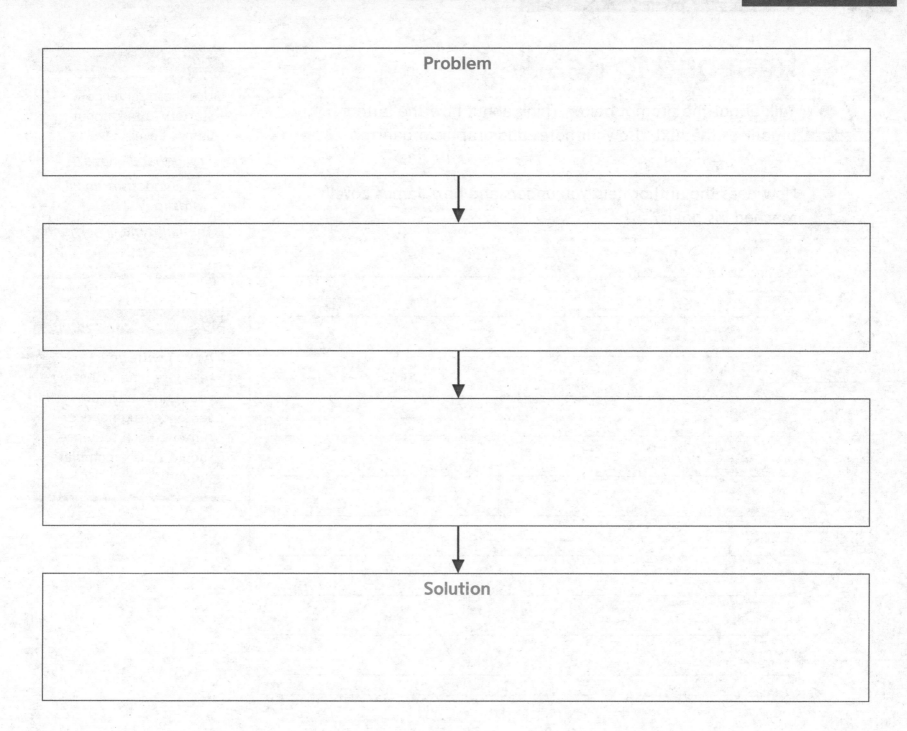

Respond to Reading

Talk about the prompt below. Think about how the author organizes the text. Use your notes and graphic organizer.

How does the author help you understand how James Lovell reached his goals?

_____

_____

_____

_____

_____

_____

_____

_____

Quick Tip

Use these sentence starters to talk about James Lovell.

I read that James . . .

The author uses signal words to . . .

This helps me understand how . . .

Grammar Connections

As you write your response, check that you do not have any sentence fragments or run-ons. Each sentence should state a complete thought.

Understanding Information

It is important to be able to demonstrate that you understand the information you gather. A **timeline** shows the order in which important events happened. Using a timeline is one way to show that you understand information.

Look at the timeline. What event happened in 1928?

_____

When did James Lovell lead the Apollo 13 space mission?

_____

James A. Lovell Meets His Goals				
1928	1952	1962	1970	1973
Born in Cleveland, Ohio	Completed training at US Naval Academy	Became an astronaut	Served as commander of the Apollo 13 space mission	Retired from the space program

COLLABORATE

Create a Timeline With a partner, gather information about someone who has worked hard to meet a goal. Use these steps and the model timeline above:

1. Identify 4 or 5 important events.
2. Put the events in the order they happened.
3. Add illustrations to your timeline.

Looking Up to Ellen Ochoa

 How does the author use text features to help you understand Ellen Ochoa's biography?

Literature Anthology: pages 462–471

 Talk About It Look at the text features on pages 464 and 465. Discuss with a partner what you learned about Ellen Ochoa.

Cite Text Evidence What do the text features help you understand? Write text evidence in the chart.

Text Feature	What It Tells Me about Ellen Ochoa
quotation	
caption	
photograph	

Write The author uses text features to help me understand

_____

_____

_____

_____

Make Inferences

Making an inference is using text evidence and what you know to make a guess about something that isn't stated in a selection. Make an inference. Reread the second paragraph on page 464. Name two people Ellen Ochoa looked up to.

How does the author use photographs and captions to help you understand that goals are important?

 Talk About It Reread the second paragraph on page 464. Turn and talk with a partner about Ellen's dream.

Cite Text Evidence What clues in the photographs and captions show how Ellen reached her goals? Write text evidence.

 Synthesize Information

The main text says the "robotic arms look like human arms." How do the text features, such as photos and captions, help you understand how a robotic arm is like a human arm?

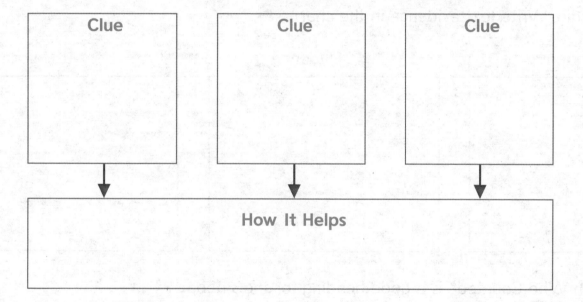

Clue	Clue	Clue

How It Helps

Write The author uses photographs and captions to help me

understand that goals are important by _____

_____

_____

? **Why is "Women Who Counted" a good heading for the sidebar?**

Talk About It Reread the sidebar on page 470. Talk with a partner about what Dorothy Vaughan, Mary Jackson, and Katherine Johnson did at NASA.

Cite Text Evidence What details tell about the women at NASA and what they did. Write text evidence in the chart.

Text Evidence	Text Evidence	How It Helps

Write "Women Who Counted" is a good heading for the sidebar

because _____

_____

_____

_____

Respond to Reading

COLLABORATE

Answer the prompt below. Think about how the author uses text features to help you learn about Ellen Ochoa and her life. Use your notes and graphic organizer.

How does the author use text features to help you understand how Ellen Ochoa reached her goals?

_____

_____

_____

_____

_____

_____

_____

_____

_____

_____

Quick Tip

Use these sentence starters to talk about the text features.

The text features help me understand . . .

The author uses photographs and captions to . . .

I know Ellen Ochoa reached her goals because . . .

Self-Selected Reading

Choose a text. Read the first two pages. If five or more words are unfamiliar, pick another text. In your writer's notebook, write the title, author, genre, and purpose for reading the book.

A Flight to Lunar City

Literature Anthology:
pages 474–475

[1] Going to the Moon had been Maria's goal since she was five. The dream had motivated Maria to enter a science project in the National Space Contest. She had invented Robbie, the robot dog, as her science project. He was the perfect Moon pet. Maria and Robbie had won first prize —a trip to Lunar City, the first settlement on the Moon.

[2] Now they were almost there! Robbie wriggled and squirmed. "Settle down!" Maria scolded. Sometimes Robbie was awfully wild, like a real puppy. Maria was thinking about adjusting his Personality Profile Program to make him a little calmer.

Reread and use the prompts to take notes in the text.

Underline words and phrases in paragraphs 1 and 2 that help you understand the setting of the story. Describe the setting here.

_____

_____

COLLABORATE

Talk with a partner about Maria's goal. **Circle** text evidence to support your discussion. Write those details here.

_____

_____

_____

_____

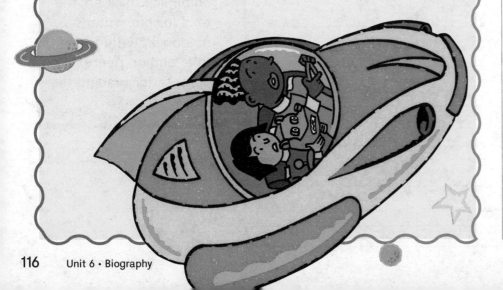

1   Just then Robbie jumped out of Maria's arms and leaped across the landing ship. He jumped onto the stick with all four paws and growled fiercely. He tugged and chewed on it. "Stop!" cried Maria.

2   All at once the control stick shifted into position. The lights came back on. The landing ship whooshed forward. "Robbie, you did it!" laughed Commander Buckley. "Good dog!" She handed Robbie back to Maria. "Now we can land on the Moon."

3   Maria smiled proudly. Robbie was the best robot dog ever!

Reread paragraph 1. **Underline** words and phrases that describe what Robbie does. **Circle** what Maria says.

COLLABORATE

Reread paragraphs 2 and 3. Talk with a partner about how Robbie solves the problem. **Draw a box around** details in the story that let you know how Commander Buckley and Maria feel. Write how they feel here.

_____

_____

_____

_____

_____

_____

_____

_____

_____

_____

How does the author use details to help you visualize how Robbie fixes the problem?

Talk About It Reread the excerpt on page 117. Talk with a partner about what Robbie does.

Cite Text Evidence What words and phrases show what Robbie does to fix the problem? Write text evidence in the chart.

Text Evidence	What I Visualize

Quick Tip

When you reread, use the author's words and phrases to help you picture in your mind what the characters do. Visualizing, or making images in your mind, helps you understand the text better.

Write I can visualize what Robbie does because the author

_____

_____

Imagery

Writers use imagery, or strong words and colorful details, to help readers form pictures in their minds as they read. Imagery helps readers understand what is happening in a story.

 FIND TEXT EVIDENCE

In the last paragraph on page 474 of "A Flight to Lunar City" in the **Literature Anthology,** *the author describes what happens to the lunar lander using phrases like* "jerked forward," "turned upside down," *and* "rolled sideways." *The author chooses strong words that help us picture what is happening.*

> Suddenly there was a large bang. The lunar lander jerked forward and turned upside down. Then it rolled sideways.

Your Turn Reread the fifth and sixth paragraphs on page 475.

- What words and phrases does the author use to help you picture what Robbie is doing? _____

  _____

- How do those words and phrases help you picture what Robbie is doing? _____

  _____

Text Connections

? **How is the message of this song similar to Ellen Ochoa's path to becoming an astronaut in _Looking Up to Ellen Ochoa_ and Maria's goals in "A Flight to Lunar City"?**

Talk About It Read the song lyrics. With a partner, talk about how you feel after reading it.

Cite Text Evidence Underline words and phrases in the lyrics that tell what the song's message is. Think about how the message makes you feel.

Write The message of this song is similar to Ellen

Ochoa's career path because _____

_____

_____

_____

_____

_____

_____

_____

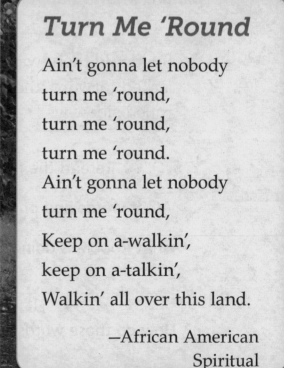

Turn Me 'Round

Ain't gonna let nobody
turn me 'round,
turn me 'round,
turn me 'round.
Ain't gonna let nobody
turn me 'round,
Keep on a-walkin',
keep on a-talkin',
Walkin' all over this land.

—African American
Spiritual

Design Pics/Bilderbuch.

Integrate | **RESEARCH AND INQUIRY**

Present Your Work

Decide how you will present your timeline to the class. Create a digital poster or make one using poster board. Use the checklist to help you improve your presentation.

1958 — She was born

1971 — She lived with her mother and three brothers and sister

1975 — She graduated from High School

1985 — She graduated from Stanford University.

1991 — She became an astronaut

Before I present, I will review my timeline to make sure that:

_____

_____

I think my presentation was _____

_____

Next time I could _____

_____

Quick Tip

Consider using a pointer to draw your audience's attention to each event on the timeline as you talk about it. Remember to face the audience and speak directly to them instead of facing your poster and reading from it.

✔ Presenting Checklist

☐ I will practice my presentation.

☐ I will point to the events on my timeline as I speak.

☐ I will make eye contact with the audience.

☐ I will speak clearly and at an appropriate rate.

☐ I will speak loud enough for everyone to hear me.

Literature Anthology:
pages 462–471

Expert Model

Features of a Research Report

A **research report** is a kind of expository text. A research report

- has an introduction that presents the main ideas

- summarizes information from more than one source on a clear central idea

- has a concluding statement or section

Analyze an Expert Model Reread page 463 of *Looking Up to Ellen Ochoa* in the **Literature Anthology**. Cite text evidence and write your answers below.

How does Liane Onish introduce the topic?

_____

_____

_____

How does the author make you want to read more? _____

_____

_____

Word Wise

Writers use linking words or phrases such as *but, although,* or *however* to connect main ideas in a research report. For example, Liane Onish says "Ellen wasn't chosen at first, but that didn't stop her." This sentence helps the text transition, or move to the next section about how Ellen worked hard to meet her goals.

Plan: Choose Your Topic

COLLABORATE

Freewrite Freewriting helps you gather your thoughts and focus your ideas. When you freewrite, you write for a short amount of time without worrying about spelling or grammar. Talk with a partner about why goals are important. Freewrite for two minutes about goals. Then make a list of people who have worked hard to meet their goals. Include astronauts, scientists, athletes, artists, and others who have shown that goals are important. Use these sentence starters to talk about your ideas.

I know goals are important because . . .

People meet their goals by . . .

Writing Prompt Choose one person from your list. Write a research report telling what that person did to reach a goal.

I will write about _____.

Purpose and Audience An author's purpose is the main reason for writing. Your audience is who will be reading it.

The reason I am writing about this person is

_____

_____

Quick Tip

Research reports are written to share information, or to inform. Research reports can be about many different things, from dinosaurs to rock stars. Strong research reports are supported by facts and carefully researched information.

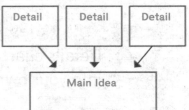

Plan In your writer's notebook, make a Main Idea and Detail chart to plan your writing. Fill in the Main Idea box.

Plan: Research

Gather Relevant Information Before you write your research report you will need to choose reliable sources for information. Encyclopedias, websites, interviews, books, and magazines are examples of reliable sources. Be sure to use information that is relevant, or closely related, to what you are writing about. Ask yourself

- Does this fact tell about the person I am writing about?
- Is the information related to the person's goal?
- Am I gathering information from more than one source?

List two pieces of relevant information you found.

1 _____

_____

2 _____

_____

 Take Notes As you research, take notes and fill in your Main Idea and Details chart. Make sure to paraphrase the information by putting it into your own words. Include only the most important information.

> **Digital Tools**
>
> For more information on how to take notes, watch "Paraphrase the Idea." Go to **my.mheducation.com**.

Draft

COLLABORATE

Develop the Topic Authors use facts, definitions, and details to develop the topic of their research report. They start with a clear central idea and use research to convey information about their topic. In the example below from "Rocketing into Space," the author uses facts to help you understand what happened on the Apollo 13 mission.

> Apollo 13 was supposed to land on the Moon. Two days after leaving Earth, however, the spacecraft had a serious problem. One of its oxygen tanks exploded. The crew did not have enough power or air to breathe. They could not make it to the Moon.

Use the above paragraph as a model to write about the person you chose for your topic. In the first sentence, tell about the main idea of the paragraph. Then develop the topic using facts and details.

_____

_____

_____

_____

Write a Draft Use your Main Idea and Details chart to help you write your draft in your writer's notebook.

Grammar Connections

Use different kinds of sentences to make your research report more interesting to read. Be sure to capitalize official titles of people and place names. For example, notice that Earth and Moon are capitalized. That's because they are proper nouns.

Revise

Voice An author's voice is the tone or feel of the research report. The author's use of language and word choice contributes to the voice. Sometimes the tone of an expository text is serious. Sometimes it is more lighthearted.

Reread the following paragraph from "Rocketing into Space." Talk with a partner about the author's voice.

> The trip back to Earth was dangerous and scary. For almost four days, the astronauts traveled in a cramped capsule. They were cold, thirsty, and hungry. Then, with millions of people watching on television, the module fell to Earth.

Is this paragraph serious or funny? What words and phrases contribute to the voice? Write about the author's voice here.

_____

_____

_____

Revise It's time to revise your writing. Read your draft and look for places where you might add words or phrases that convey emotion, or voice.

_____

Quick Tip

When you revise, make sure your research report is clearly organized. Does your introduction name the person and his or her goal? Do main ideas and details support the topic? Does your conclusion sum up the report?

Peer Conferences

Review a Draft Listen carefully as a partner reads his or her draft aloud. Tell what you like about the draft. Use these sentence starters to help you discuss your partner's draft.

I like this part because it helped me to understand . . .

I have a question about . . .

Add another fact or detail here to . . .

Partner Feedback After you take turns giving each other feedback, write one of the suggestions from your partner that you will use in your revision.

_____

_____

_____

_____

Revision After you finish your peer conference, use the Revising Checklist to help you figure out what you can change to make your research report better. Remember to use the rubric on page 129 to help you with your revision.

Revising Checklist

☐ Does my introduction clearly introduce the person I researched?

☐ Do I include main ideas and details about how the person reached a goal?

☐ Is my report written in an appropriate voice?

☐ Did I use at least two resources to find relevant information for my report?

Tech Tip

By typing your report on a computer, you can make revisions more easily. You can insert new details or rearrange paragraphs without having to rewrite your report.

Edit and Proofread

When you **edit** and **proofread** your writing, you look for and correct mistakes in grammar, spelling, and punctuation. Read your draft at least three times. This will help you catch any mistakes. Use the checklist below to edit your sentences.

Grammar Connections

When you proofread your draft for mistakes, remember to look for words that compare people, things, or even groups as in, "Since most astronauts were men, Ellen Ochoa had to work even *harder*."

✔ Editing Checklist

☐ Do all sentences begin with a capital letter and end with a punctuation mark?

☐ Are there capital letters at the beginning of proper nouns?

☐ Are adjectives that compare used correctly?

☐ Are all the words spelled correctly?

List two mistakes that you found as you proofread your research report.

1 _____

_____

_____

2 _____

_____

_____

Publish, Present, and Evaluate

Publishing When you **publish** your writing, you create a neat, final copy that is free of mistakes. If you are not using a computer, use your best handwriting. Write legibly in print or cursive.

Presentation When you are ready to present, practice your presentation. Use the presenting checklist.

Evaluate After you publish, use the rubric to **evaluate** it.

What did you do successfully? _____

_____

What needs more work? _____

_____

✓ Presenting Checklist

☐ Look at the audience.

☐ Speak slowly and clearly.

☐ Stand up straight.

☐ Answer questions thoughtfully.

4	3	2	1
• well focused on topic; many supporting details • appropriate voice used in all parts • provides a strong beginning and a strong conclusion	• mostly focused on topic; some supporting details • appropriate voice used in most parts • beginning and conclusion are missing a key detail	• partly focused on topic; few supporting details • inappropriate voice used in some parts • beginning and conclusion are missing facts and details	• topic not focused; no supporting details • inappropriate voice used throughout • weak beginning and conclusion

Spending time with her grandfather is important to Brianna. He shares what he knows and helps her learn new things. Sharing, learning new things, and healthy habits are all important to Brianna.

Look at the photograph. What new thing is Brianna learning? Write four things that you value, or are important, in the word web.

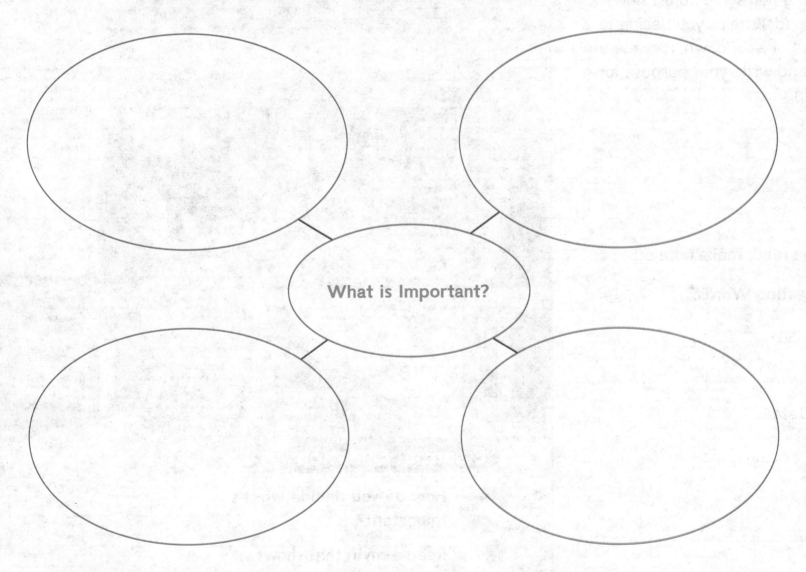

What is Important?

Go online to **my.mheducation.com** and read the "Snow Leopards" Blast. Think about how people decide what is important. Then blast back your response.

TAKE NOTES

Understanding why you are reading helps you adjust how you read. It helps you decide to reread or slow down. Preview the text and write your purpose for reading here.

_____

_____

_____

As you read, make note of:

Interesting Words: _____

_____

_____

Key Details: _____

_____

_____

_____

_____

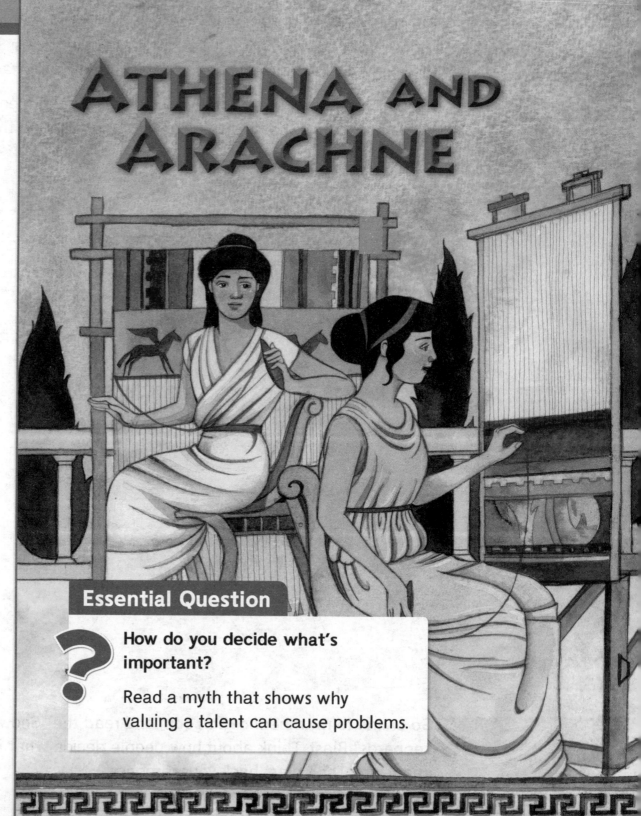

ATHENA AND ARACHNE

Essential Question

? **How do you decide what's important?**

Read a myth that shows why valuing a talent can cause problems.

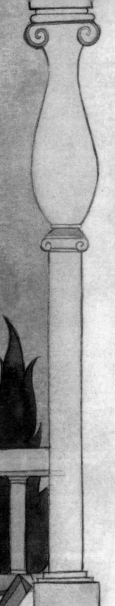

CHARACTERS

NARRATOR

ARACHNE: (uh-RAK-nee)

DIANA: Arachne's friend

ATHENA: a Greek goddess

MESSENGER

⟶ SCENE ONE ⟵

Athens, Greece, a long time ago, Arachne's home.

NARRATOR: Long ago, Arachne and her friend Diana sat weaving.

DIANA: Oh, Arachne! That cloth is so beautiful.

Arachne admires her cloth.

ARACHNE: I know. Many people want to **possess** my cloth, but few can afford it. Only those with great **wealth** can buy it.

DIANA: Yes, it's true that people value your cloth. It is one of their most valued possessions. Your weavings are a real **treasure.** Some say that you learned your weaving skill, or talent, from the goddess Athena.

ARACHNE: It was not **necessary** for me to learn from a goddess. I was born with my talent. I am a much better weaver than Athena, and I'm sure I could beat her in a weaving competition!

Diana is worried, stops weaving and looks at Arachne.

DIANA: Ssshhh! I hope Athena isn't listening, or you're in big trouble!

ARACHNE: Nonsense! There's no reason to be **alarmed** or worried. Athena is much too busy to come down from Mount Olympus to compete with me.

Jenny Reynish

FIND TEXT EVIDENCE

Read

Scene One

Theme

Circle what Diana says to Arachne at the beginning of Scene One.

Scene One

Stage Directions

Draw boxes around the stage directions in Scene One.

Scene One

Make Predictions

Read Arachne's last line in Scene One. What prediction can you make about Athena?

_____

_____

_____

Reread

Author's Craft

How does the author use dialogue to help you understand what Arachne is like?

SHARED READ

FIND TEXT EVIDENCE

Read

Scene Two

Confirm Predictions

Check the prediction you made on page 133. **Circle** clues.

Scene Two

Root Words

Draw a box around the word *apologize*. Write the root word here.

Scene Three

Dialogue

How does Athena trick Arachne?

Underline text evidence.

Reread

Author's Craft

How does the author use stage directions to help you understand what the characters are doing?

⇛ SCENE TWO ⇚

Mount Olympus, home of Athena. A messenger arrives.

MESSENGER: Goddess Athena! I have news from Athens. The weaver Arachne says she can beat you in a weaving competition. She is **obsessed** with her skill and thinks she is the best weaver in Greece!

ATHENA: I'll show her who weaves the finest cloth! Her obsession with weaving must end. Please get me my cloak. *Messenger hands Athena her cloak.*

ATHENA: Arachne cannot talk about me that way! If she refuses to apologize, I will make her pay for her boastful words. Her **anguish** will be great!

⇛ SCENE THREE ⇚

Arachne's home. There is a knock at the door.

ARACHNE: Who's there?

ATHENA: Just an old woman with a question.

Athena is hiding under her cloak. She enters the room.

ATHENA: Is it true that you challenged the goddess Athena to a weaving competition?

ARACHNE: Yes, that's right. *Athena drops her cloak.*

ATHENA: Well, I am Athena. I am here to compete with you!

DIANA: Arachne, please don't! It is unwise to compete with a goddess!

Arachne and Athena sit down at the empty looms and begin to weave furiously.

ARACHNE: I am ready to win and get my reward!

ATHENA: There's no prize if you lose!

NARRATOR: Arachne and Athena both wove beautiful cloths. However, Arachne's cloth was filled with pictures of the gods being unkind.

ATHENA: Arachne, your weaving is beautiful, but I am insulted and upset by the pictures you chose to weave. You are boastful, and your cloth is mean and unkind. For that, I will punish you.

Athena points dramatically at Arachne. Arachne falls behind her loom and crawls out as a spider.

ATHENA: Arachne, you will spend the rest of your life weaving and living in your own web.

NARRATOR: Arachne was mean and boastful, so Athena turned her into a spider. That's why spiders are now called arachnids. Arachne learned that bragging and too much pride can lead to trouble.

⟢ **THE END** ⟣

Summarize

Use your notes to share the theme of "Athena and Arachne" with a partner. Summarize which parts of the story helped create the theme. Talk about whether your prediction on page 133 was confirmed.

FIND TEXT EVIDENCE

Read

Scene Three
Make Predictions

Make a prediction about who will win the contest. **Underline** clues that helped you guess.

Scene Three
Dialogue

Why is Athena insulted and upset by Arachne's weaving?

_____

_____

Draw a box around text evidence.

Reread

Author's Craft

How does the author help you understand how something came to be?

Vocabulary

Use the sentences to talk with a partner about each word. Then answer the questions.

alarmed

Jess was **alarmed** as she saw her basketball bounce over the fence.

Describe how you would look if you were alarmed by something.

_____

_____

anguish

Andy felt **anguish** when he realized his bike was missing.

What is another word that means the same as anguish?

_____

_____

necessary

Food is **necessary** for all living things.

What other things are necessary for living things?

_____

_____

obsessed

Victor is **obsessed** with space and is saving for a telescope.

Name something you are obsessed with.

_____

_____

possess

Dan and Meg **possess** a huge bunch of colorful pencils.

Tell about something you possess.

_____

_____

 Build Your Word List Look back at the list of interesting words you noted on page 132. Choose one and use a word web to write more forms of the word. Use an online or print dictionary to help you find more related words.

reward

Mom made my favorite dinner as a **reward** for passing my math test.

What reward would you like to get?

_____

_____

treasure

Lila found a real **treasure** at the book sale.

Tell about a treasure you have.

_____

_____

wealth

We are counting our coins to see how much **wealth** we have.

What is another word for wealth?

_____

_____

_____

Root Words

A root word is the simplest form of a word. It helps you figure out the meaning of a related word.

🔍 **FIND TEXT EVIDENCE**

In "Athena and Arachne," I see the word competition. *I think the root word of* competition *is* compete. *I know* compete *means "to try to win" I think* competition *is "a contest where people try to win."*

I am a much better weaver than Athena, and I'm sure I could beat her in a weaving competition!

Your Turn Find the root word. Then use it to figure out the meaning of the word.

possessions, page 133 _____

_____

_____

Make Predictions

Use details in the story to predict what happens next. Read on to confirm, or check it. Correct your prediction if it is not right.

 FIND TEXT EVIDENCE

You may have made a prediction about Arachne. What clues on page 133 helped you guess what might happen?

Quick Tip

Read on to confirm, or check your prediction. If your prediction is not correct, find text evidence and revise it.

> Page 133
>
> **DIANA:** Oh, Arachne! That cloth is so beautiful.
>
> *Arachne admires her cloth.*
>
> **ARACHNE:** I know. Many people want to **possess** my cloth, but few can afford it. Only those with great **wealth** can buy it.
>
> **DIANA:** Yes, it's true that people value your cloth. It is one of their most valued possessions. Your weavings are a real **treasure.** Some say that you learned your weaving skill, or talent, from the goddess Athena.
>
> **ARACHNE:** It was not **necessary** for me to learn from a goddess. I was born with my talent. I am a much better weaver than Athena, and I'm sure I could beat her in a weaving competition!

I predicted that Arachne and Athena would compete. I read that Arachne says she is a better weaver than Athena and could beat her in a contest. I will read on to confirm, or check my prediction.

 Your Turn What did you predict would happen when Athena went to see Arachne? Reread page 134 to confirm your prediction. Write your prediction here and the text evidence that supports it or changes it.

_____

_____

Stage Directions and Dialogue

"Athena and Arachne" is a myth and a drama, or play. A myth tells how something came to be. A **drama**

- tells a story through dialogue and is performed
- is separated into acts with different scenes and has stage directions

Readers to Writers

An act is a group of scenes in a drama. Writers use the act to tell big parts of the story, such as the beginning, middle, and end. When you write a play, think about how your scenes work together to tell the whole story.

FIND TEXT EVIDENCE

I see that "Athena and Arachne" is a myth and a play. It is divided into three scenes. The play uses dialogue and stage directions to tell how spiders came to weave webs.

Page 134

⇒⊛ SCENE TWO ⊛⇐

Mount Olympus, home of Athena. A messenger arrives.

MESSENGER: Goddess Athena! I have news from Athens. The weaver Arachne says she can beat you in a weaving competition. She is **obsessed** with her skill and thinks she is the best weaver in Greece!

ATHENA: I'll show her who weaves the finest cloth! Her obsession with weaving must end. Please get me my cloak.
Messenger hands Athena her cloak.

ATHENA: Arachne cannot talk about me that way! If she refuses to apologize, I will make her pay for her boastful words. Her **anguish** will be great!

⇒⊛ SCENE THREE ⊛⇐

Arachne's home. There is a knock at the door.

ARACHNE: Who's there?

ATHENA: Just an old woman with a question.
Athena is hiding under her cloak. She enters the room.

ATHENA: Is it true that you challenged the goddess Athena to a weaving competition?

ARACHNE: Yes, that's right. *Athena drops her cloak.*

ATHENA: Well, I am Athena. I am here to compete with you!

DIANA: Arachne, please don't! It is unwise to compete with a goddess!

Arachne and Athena sit down at the empty looms and begin

Scene
A scene is a part of a play. Scenes tell the story in time order.

Stage Directions
Stage directions tell what the characters do and how they move.

Dialogue
Dialogue is the words the characters speak.

Your Turn Find one example of dialogue and stage directions in "Athena and Arachne." Write them here.

_____

_____

Theme

The theme of a story is the author's message. Think about what the characters do and say. This will help you infer, or figure out, the theme.

FIND TEXT EVIDENCE

In "Athena and Arachne," Arachne learns that bragging and too much pride can lead to trouble. This is the story's theme. I can reread to find details that help me infer, or figure out, the theme.

Detail
Arachne said that many people want to possess her cloth, but few can afford it. Only those with great wealth can buy it.

↓

Detail

↓

Detail

↓

Detail

↓

Theme
Bragging and too much pride can lead to trouble.

Your Turn Reread "Athena and Arachne." List important details about what Arachne says and does in your graphic organizer. Be sure the details tell about the theme.

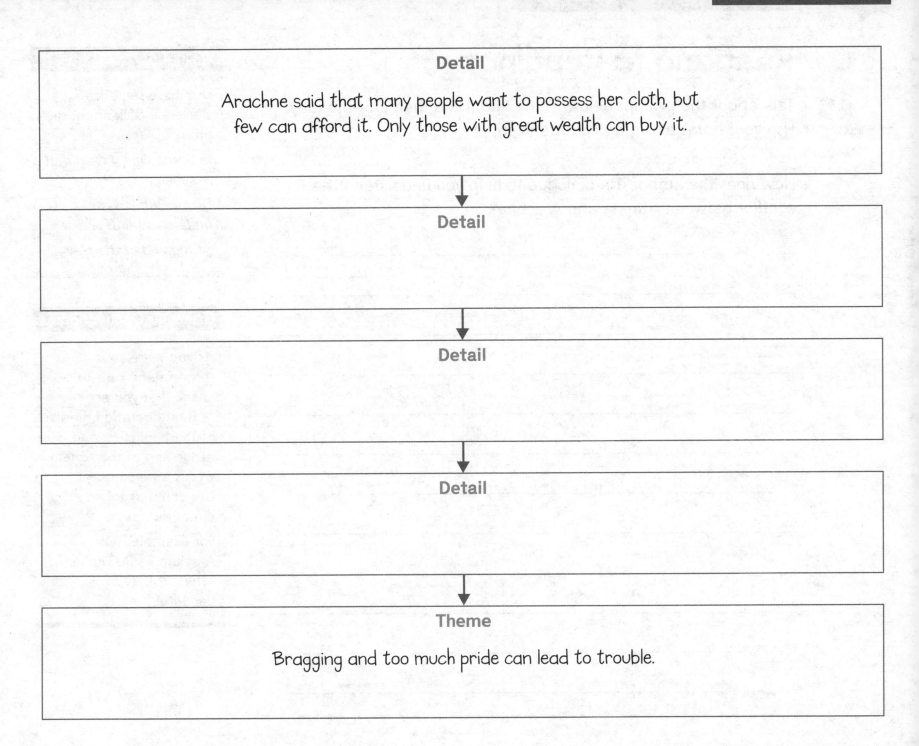

Detail

Arachne said that many people want to possess her cloth, but few can afford it. Only those with great wealth can buy it.

Detail

Detail

Detail

Theme

Bragging and too much pride can lead to trouble.

Respond to Reading

COLLABORATE

Talk about the prompt below. Think about the theme of the play. Use your notes and graphic organizer.

How does the author use dialogue to help you understand the conflict between Athena and Arachne?

_____

_____

_____

_____

_____

_____

_____

_____

_____

_____

_____

Using Information

One way to gather information is to ask questions. One way to show that you understand information is to share it. A bar graph is a special kind of picture. It helps you understand numbers and information in a quick and easy way.

Look at the bar graph. What is the title?

_____

What quality is the most important?

_____

Create a Bar Graph With a partner, make a bar graph about something that is important to you. Use these steps.

1. Think of a question that has four possible answers to ask classmates. Write the question here.

_____

2. Draw a bar graph and write a title. Write the four answers along the bottom.

3. Ask 6 classmates your question. Tell them the answer choices. Record their answers on your bar graph. Discuss the results with your partner. After you finish, you will share them with the class.

Quick Tip

Think about what's important to you and your classmates. Is it taking care of your pets? Spending time with friends and family? Eating healthful snacks? Pick one topic and find out what others think is important.

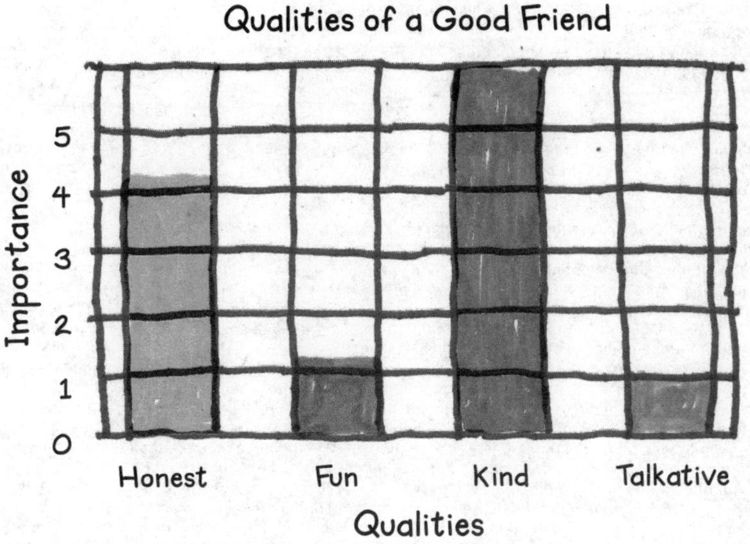

Qualities of a Good Friend

(Bar graph: y-axis labeled "Importance" from 0 to 5; x-axis labeled "Qualities" with Honest, Fun, Kind, Talkative)

King Midas and the Golden Touch

? How does the author help you visualize how much King Midas loves gold?

Literature Anthology: pages 476–489

Talk About It Reread pages 478 and 479 and look at the illustration. With a partner, talk about what King Midas does.

Cite Text Evidence What words, phrases, and images help to show how King Midas feels about gold? Write text evidence in the web.

 Synthesize Information

Look for text evidence that shows characters' words and actions. Then draw a conclusion about how much King Midas loves gold.

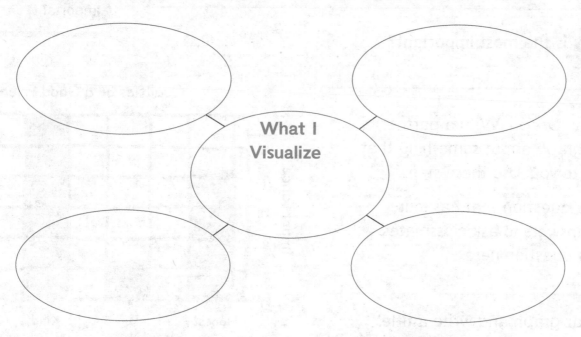

What I Visualize

Write I can picture how much Midas loves gold because the author

_____

_____

? **How does the author show that King Midas is not just interested in gold?**

Talk About It Reread page 482. Talk with a partner about the gift that King Midas gives Marigold.

Cite Text Evidence What clues help you see that King Midas is interested in more than his money? Write text evidence in the chart.

Clue

Clue

Clue

What It Shows

Write The author shows that King Midas cares about other things by

_____

_____

? **How does the author show that something might happen to Marigold later in the story?**

Talk About It Reread page 485. Talk with a partner about what happens to the stone and the rose.

Cite Text Evidence What clues show that something might happen to Marigold? Write text evidence.

Make Inferences

Think about what you already know and the author's words and phrases. Then make an inference about what might happen between Marigold and her father later in the story.

Clue

↓

Clue

↓

Clue

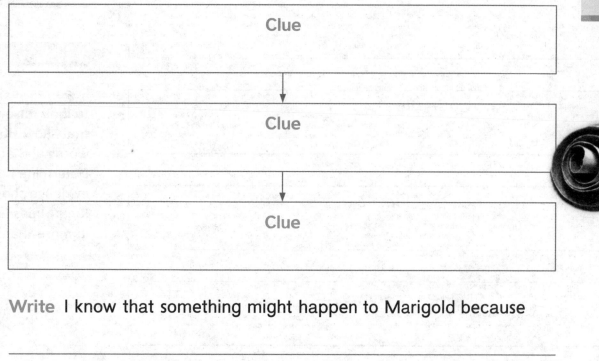

Write I know that something might happen to Marigold because

_____

_____

_____

Respond to Reading

Answer the prompt below. Think about how the author's words and phrases develop the play's theme. Use your notes and graphic organizer.

How does the author help you understand the theme of this play?

_____

_____

_____

_____

_____

_____

_____

_____

_____

_____

_____

Quick Tip

Use these sentence starters to talk about the theme of the play.

The author uses sensory language to describe how King Midas . . .

She also compares . . .

This helps me understand the theme because . . .

Self-Selected Reading

Choose a text. In your writer's notebook, write the title, author, and genre of the book. As you read, make a connection to ideas in other texts you have read or to a personal experience. Write your ideas in your notebook.

Carlos's Gift

Literature Anthology: pages 492–495

1   Carlos wanted a puppy in the worst way. He dreamed about puppies—big ones, little ones, spotted ones, frisky ones. Now it was his birthday, and Carlos had one thing on his mind. A puppy! When Mama handed him a flat, square box, Carlos almost started to cry.

2   It was a book about caring for dogs.

3   Papa smiled, "You need to learn how to care for a puppy before you get one."

4   Carlos read the book that night. He found a photograph of the exact kind of bulldog puppy that he craved. He eagerly showed Mama the next morning.

Reread and use the prompts to take notes in the text.

Underline phrases in paragraph 1 that show how much Carlos wanted a puppy. **Circle** clues that show how he feels when Mama gives him his present. Write text evidence here:

_____

_____

_____

COLLABORATE

Reread paragraph 4. Talk with a partner about what Carlos does. **Draw a box** around two phrases that show how Carlos feels about learning to care for a dog.

1   Carlos started working at the shelter on Saturday. His assignment was sweeping. Afterwards, the dogs scampered out to play. One dog named Pepper had a funny curly tail that never stopped wagging. She was fully grown but as playful as a puppy. When Pepper leaped in the pile of stick and leaves that Carlos had just swept up, he laughed.

2   Carlos went to the shelter every weekend. He began to treasure his time with the dogs, especially Pepper. One day Carlos asked why Pepper was still at the shelter.

3   Miss Jones sighed, "We've had trouble finding a home for Pepper. Most people don't want such an energetic dog."

4   Carlos suddenly realized he didn't want a bulldog puppy. He wanted Pepper. "I wish I could buy her," he replied.

In paragraph 1, **draw a box** around words and phrases that describe Pepper. **Underline** the text evidence in paragraph 3 that tells why Pepper has not found a home. Write it here:

_____

_____

COLLABORATE

Reread the rest of the excerpt. Talk with a partner about what Miss Jones and Carlos say about Pepper. **Circle** text evidence to support your discussion.

? **How does the author use dialogue to show how Carlos feels about Pepper?**

Talk About It Reread paragraphs 2–4 on page 493. Talk with a partner about how Carlos reacts to what Miss Jones says.

Cite Text Evidence What does Carlos think and say about Pepper? Write text evidence in the chart.

 Make Inferences

Read the dialogue carefully to make an inference about how Carlos feels.

Text Evidence	How Carlos Feels

Write I know how Carlos feels about Pepper because the author uses

dialogue to _____

_____

Problem and Solution

Writers organize information in ways to help the reader understand their writing. One way to organize the text is by problem and solution. The writer introduces a problem. Then shows how the problem is solved.

🔍 FIND TEXT EVIDENCE

*In paragraph 3 on page 494 of "Carlos's Gift" in the **Literature Anthology** the author uses the phrase "We've had trouble." This shows that there is a problem. By telling us about the problem, the author helps us know to look for a solution.*

> Miss Jones sighed, "We've had trouble finding a home for Pepper. Most people don't want such an energetic dog."

Your Turn Reread the first two paragraphs on page 495.

- How does the author use dialogue to help you understand what
  Carlos must do to solve the problem? _____

  _____

- How do you know how Carlos feels? _____

  _____

Readers to Writers

Organize your writing by problem and solution to show your readers how a character solves a problem or overcomes an obstacle.

Text Connections

? **How does the photographer of the picture below show what is important? How is this the same as what the authors do in *King Midas and the Golden Touch* and "Carlos's Gift"?**

Talk About It Look at the photograph and read the caption. Talk with a partner about what you see happening in the photograph.

Cite Text Evidence Circle clues that show how Chloe is helping. Underline the words in the caption that tell what Chloe is doing. Draw a box around the part of the photograph that helps you know how Chloe feels.

Write The photographer shows what's

important by _____

_____

_____

_____

_____

Chloe is always busy, but she volunteers at the food bank every week.

Quick Tip

You can tell what someone thinks is important by looking at their actions. Look at what Chloe is doing to understand what she thinks is important.

Present Your Work

Decide how you will present your information to the class. Create an online presentation or a digital poster. Use the checklist to help you improve your presentation.

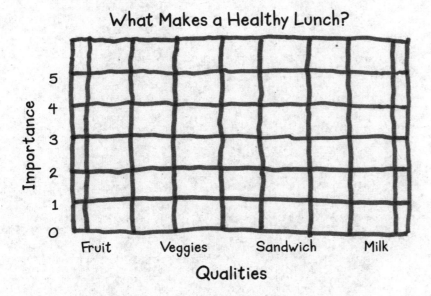

What Makes a Healthy Lunch?

(y-axis) Importance: 5, 4, 3, 2, 1, 0

(x-axis) Fruit, Veggies, Sandwich, Milk

Qualities

Before I present, I will review the information to make sure I understand it. Then I will explain my bar graph and what it means.

I think my presentation was _____.

I know because _____

_____

_____

Tech Tip

Word processors and spreadsheet programs allow you to insert a bar graph and display your information. Look for Menu options labeled Charts.

✓ **Presenting Checklist**

☐ I will review my information.

☐ I will practice my presentation.

☐ I will speak clearly.

☐ I will point to the information in the graph.

☐ I will discuss what I learned.

Essential Question

What makes you laugh?

Lots of things make you laugh—jokes, funny stories, silly pictures. Having a good sense of humor is important. Laughing makes you feel good. Laughing helps you share feelings with friends.

Just look at these pink pigs. Talk about what you think is humorous about them. Then write what makes you laugh in the word web.

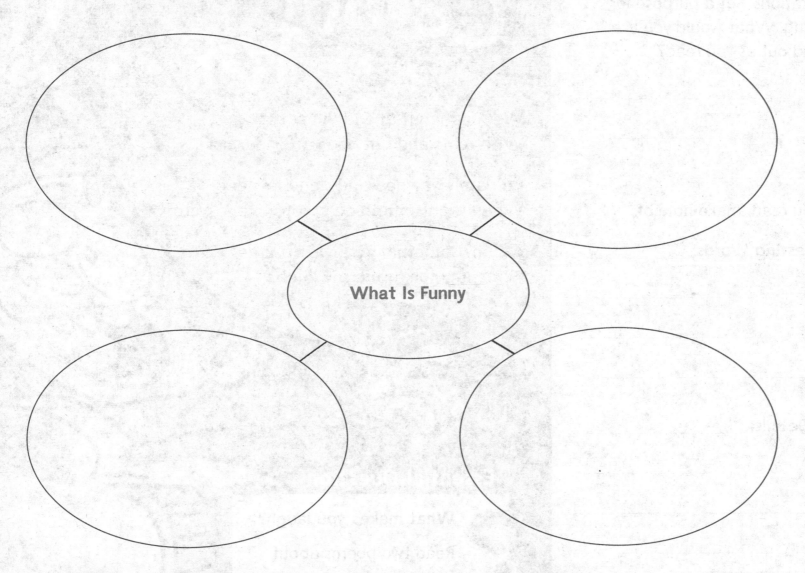

What Is Funny

 BLAST BACK! studysync Go online to **my.mheducation.com** and read the "The Best Medicine" Blast. Think about how you feel when you laugh. Then blast back your response.

SHARED READ

TAKE NOTES

Preview the poems and the illustrations. Set a purpose for reading. What would you like to find out as you read?

As you read, make note of:

Interesting Words:

Key Details:

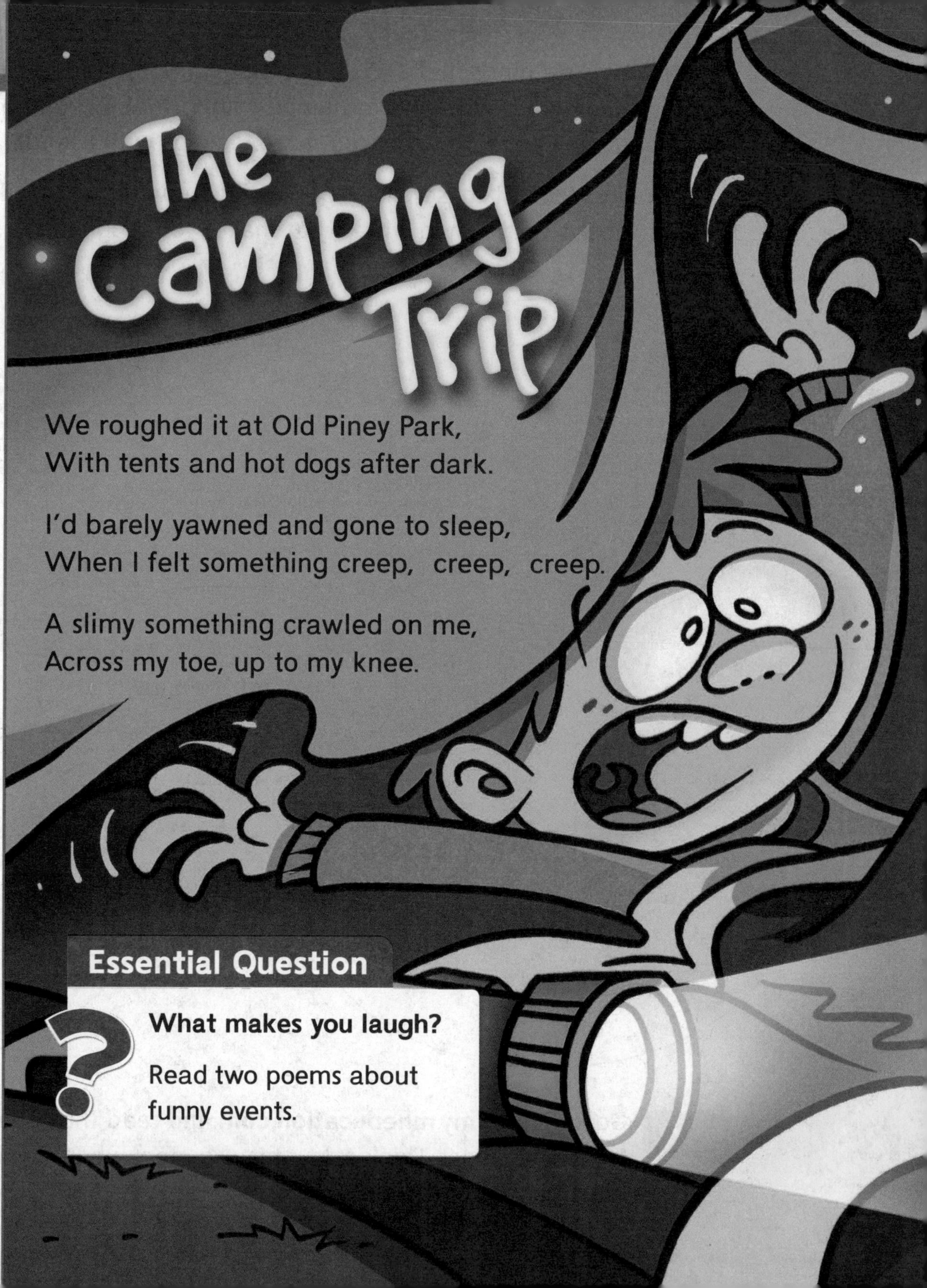

The Camping Trip

We roughed it at Old Piney Park,
With tents and hot dogs after dark.

I'd barely yawned and gone to sleep,
When I felt something creep, creep, creep.

A slimy something crawled on me,
Across my toe, up to my knee.

Essential Question

What makes you laugh?

Read two poems about funny events.

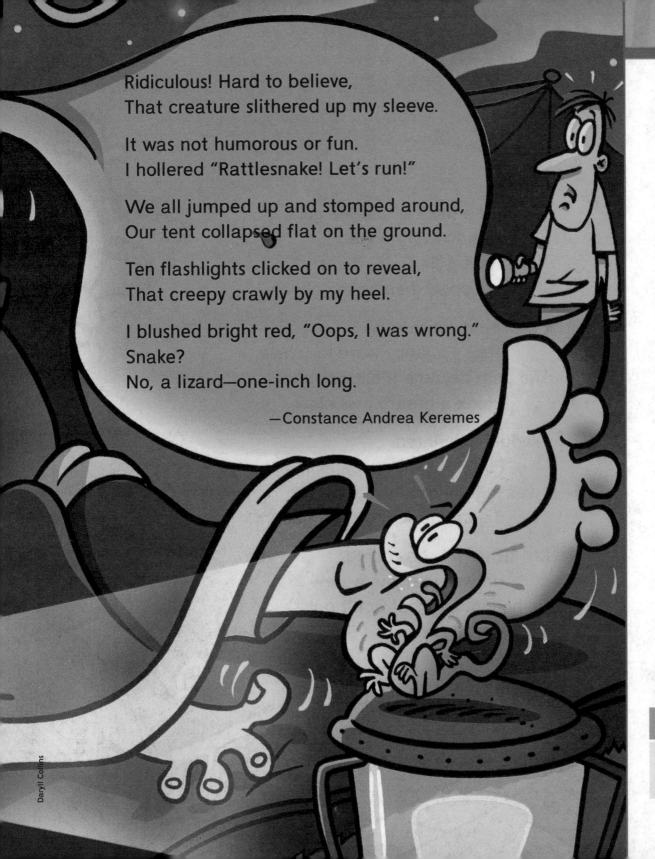

Ridiculous! Hard to believe,
That creature slithered up my sleeve.

It was not humorous or fun.
I hollered "Rattlesnake! Let's run!"

We all jumped up and stomped around,
Our tent collapsed flat on the ground.

Ten flashlights clicked on to reveal,
That creepy crawly by my heel.

I blushed bright red, "Oops, I was wrong."
Snake?
No, a lizard—one-inch long.

—Constance Andrea Keremes

Daryll Collins

FIND TEXT EVIDENCE

Read

Page 156
Stanzas
How many lines does the first stanza have?

_____

Page 156
Rhyme
Circle words that rhyme in the second stanza. Write two words that rhyme in the third stanza.

_____

Page 157
Point of View
What does the narrator think when he finds out what was crawling on him?

_____

Underline text evidence.

Reread

Author's Craft

How does the poet help you see how the narrator feels?

FIND TEXT EVIDENCE 🔍

Read

Page 158

Point of View

How does the narrator feel about bubble gum?

_____

_____

Draw a box around the text evidence.

Page 158

Idioms

Underline two idioms in the fourth stanza. Write what they mean here.

_____

_____

Reread

Author's Craft

How does the poet help you understand what _inflated_ means?

Bubble Gum

I bought a pack of bubble gum,
    As I do every week,
Unwrapping 10 or 20 sticks,
    I popped them in my cheek.

I started masticating,
    That's a fancy word for chew,
The gum became a juicy gob,
    I took a breath and blew.

I suddenly inflated,
    Puffing up like a balloon,
I was a giant bubble,
    Big and round as a full moon.

My father hit the ceiling,
    He was really in a stew,
He hollered, "Stop! Don't go!"
    As out the door I flew.

The neighbors' eyes were popping.
    They dropped everything to see.
I was the entertainment of the day.
    Forget about TV.

If you like bubble gum, beware—
    Chew just one stick a day,
Or you'll become a bubble, too
And float up   Up   AWAY!

I saw my friends below me,
    And let loose a mighty roar.
WHOOSH!
All my air blew out,
    And I was just a kid once more.

— Diana Kent

Make Connections

Which poem has the funniest events
or characters?

Daryll Collins

FIND TEXT EVIDENCE

Read

Page 159
Point of View

How do the neighbors feel about
the narrator's adventure? **Draw
a box around** the text evidence.

Page 159
Idioms

Underline the idiom in the third
stanza. Write what it means.

Fluency

With a partner, choral read the
last two stanzas on page 158.
Follow the punctuation to show
your excitement.

Reread
Author's Craft

How does the narrator help you
understand how she feels at the
end of the poem?

Vocabulary

Use the sentences to talk with a partner about each word. Then answer the questions.

entertainment

Grandpa and Devon think playing chess is great **entertainment**.

What do you like to do for entertainment?

_____

_____

humorous

Evan couldn't stop laughing at Nick's **humorous** story.

Describe a humorous time when you couldn't stop laughing.

_____

_____

ridiculous

Jess wore a **ridiculous** clown nose and made his friends giggle.

What's another word for *ridiculous*?

slithered

The long, thin snake **slithered** across the floor.

What does *slithered* mean?

_____

_____

Poetry Words

narrative poem

My favorite **narrative poem** tells about Paul Revere's ride.

What story would you tell in a narrative poem?

_____

_____

rhyme

The words *moon* and *spoon* **rhyme** because they end in the same sound.

Write two words that rhyme with *moon* and *spoon*.

_____

_____

rhythm

Ben's poem has a **rhythm** that sounds like a drumbeat.

Why might a poet include rhythm in a poem?

_____

_____

stanza

Each **stanza** in Maggie's poem has five lines.

How can you tell how many stanzas a poem has?

_____

_____

Build Your Word List Reread the fourth stanza on page 157. Draw a box around the word *reveal*. In your writer's notebook, make a list of synonyms and a list of antonyms for *reveal*. Use a thesaurus to help you add to each list.

Idioms

An idiom is a group of words that means something different from the usual meaning of each word in it. The phrase *lend a hand* is an idiom. It doesn't mean "to give someone your hand." It means "to help someone do something."

FIND TEXT EVIDENCE

On page 156 of "The Camping Trip," the phrase roughed it *is an idiom. I can use clues to figure out that it means "to live without the usual comforts of home."*

We _roughed it_ at Old Piney Park,
With tents and hot dogs after dark.

Your Turn Figure out the meaning of this idiom.

eyes were popping, page 159

_____

_____

Rhythm and Rhyme

Poets use rhythm and rhyme to make a poem interesting to listen to and fun to read.

🔍 FIND TEXT EVIDENCE

Reread the poem "Bubble Gum" on pages 158–159 aloud. Listen for words that rhyme. Clap your hands as you read the poem to follow the poem's rhythm.

Page 158

I bought a pack of bubble gum,
    As I do every week,
Unwrapping 10 or 20 sticks,
    I popped them in my cheek.

I started masticating,
    That's a fancy word for chew,
The gum became a juicy gob,
    I took a breath and blew.

Quick Tip

Read poems aloud slowly and clap for each syllable to listen for the rhythm. Pause at the end of each line before moving on to the next. Listen for rhymes at the end of lines and in the middle of lines.

In the second and fourth lines of the poem, the words week and cheek rhyme. I clapped my hands to find the rhythm. I like the way the poem has a pattern of sounds that repeat themselves.

Your Turn Reread "The Camping Trip" on pages 156–157 to find more examples of rhythm and rhyme.

_____

_____

_____

_____

_____

Stanzas and Events

Narrative poetry tells a story. It can have any number of lines and stanzas.

A **stanza** is a group of lines that form part of a poem. It often has rhyme and rhythm.

 FIND TEXT EVIDENCE

I can tell that "Bubble Gum" is a narrative poem. It tells a story. It also has stanzas. Each stanza has four lines. The second and fourth lines rhyme.

Page 158

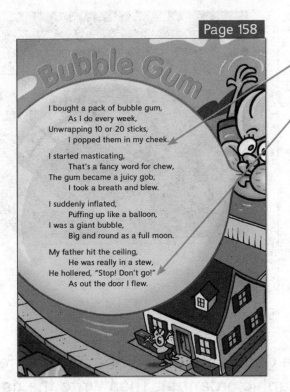

I bought a pack of bubble gum,
    As I do every week,
Unwrapping 10 or 20 sticks,
    I popped them in my cheek.

I started masticating,
    That's a fancy word for chew,
The gum became a juicy gob,
    I took a breath and blew.

I suddenly inflated,
    Puffing up like a balloon,
I was a giant bubble,
    Big and round as a full moon.

My father hit the ceiling,
    He was really in a stew,
He hollered, "Stop! Don't go!"
    As out the door I flew.

This is a stanza. It is a group of lines. There are four stanzas on this page.

The poem describes a series of events. It tells a story.

Your Turn Reread the poem "The Camping Trip." Explain why it is a narrative poem. Tell how many stanzas are in it. Write your answer below.

_____

_____

_____

Readers to Writers

Look at the series of events in "Bubble Gum." What happens at the beginning of the poem? What happens at the end?

When you write, think about what will happen first, next, and last in your poem.

Point of View

Point of view in a poem is what the narrator thinks about an event, a thing, or a person. Look for details in the poem that show the narrator's point of view.

🔍 FIND TEXT EVIDENCE

In "The Camping Trip," I read that the narrator feels something creeping on him. He calls it slimy. He says it slithered. The details tell me he is either afraid of or dislikes small, creepy crawly things. This is the narrator's point of view.

Details
"A slimy something crawled on me,"

↓

Point of View

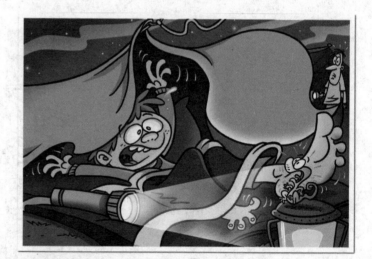

Your Turn Reread "The Camping Trip." Find more details about how the narrator feels about the creepy creature. Write them in the graphic organizer. Then write the narrator's point of view. Do you agree with his point of view? Explain in the bottom box.

Daryll Collins

Details

↓

Point of View

Respond to Reading

COLLABORATE

Talk about the prompt below. Think about how the characters in the poems feel. Use your notes and graphic organizer.

How do the poets help you understand how the narrator in each poem feels?

_____

_____

_____

_____

_____

_____

_____

_____

_____

_____

Quick Tip

Use these sentence starters to talk about the prompt.

The poets use ...

This helps me understand that ...

Grammar Connections

As you write your response, be sure to put direct quotes from the poem in quotation marks.

Hyperbole

A tall tale is a story that has larger-than-life characters, including a hero. It tells about an event that couldn't happen in real life. Writers use **hyperbole** to make their tall tales humorous, or funny.

A hyperbole is an obvious exaggeration. For example

- Jake had a ton of homework to do
- Julia was so strong she could lift a house

Read this paragraph. Circle one hyperbole. Write one on the lines.

> Once, in Florida, a baby girl was born. That night was so windy that all the mountains blew away. Well, some of that wind must have blown into that baby girl. From the time she was knee-high to a tadpole, she could control the wind with her breath alone.

_____

_____

Write a Tall Tale With a partner, read two or three tall tales. Then write a short tall tale. Remember to

1. make your hero stronger, braver, or more clever than the other characters
2. choose fun and exciting words and phrases to describe events that could not really happen
3. use at least two examples of hyperbole

Share your tall tale with your partner.

Quick Tip

Tall tales are fun to read. Johnny Appleseed, Paul Bunyan, Pecos Bill, and Windy Gale are a few examples of heroes in tall tales. Look on pages 434 and 435 in the **Literature Anthology** to read "Windy Gale and the Great Hurricane."

Ollie's Escape

  How does the poet use words and phrases to make the poem funny?

Literature Anthology: pages 496–498

 Talk About It Reread page 497. Look at the illustration. Talk with a partner about what makes this poem funny.

Cite Text Evidence What words and phrases make the poem funny? Write text evidence in the chart.

Text Evidence	How It Helps

Make Inferences

Poets often use words based on their sounds more than their meaning. You can infer what the poet means by looking at the context. What inference can you make about the meaning of "squiggled" as it is used in the poem?

Write The poet uses words and phrases to make the poem funny by

_____

_____

? **How does the poet use idioms to help you visualize the characters' actions?**

Talk About It Reread pages 497–498. Talk with a partner about what Principal Poole does when he sees Ollie.

Cite Text Evidence What words and phrases help you visualize the characters' actions? Write text evidence in the chart.

Idiom	What I Visualize

Write The author uses idioms to describe the characters' actions to

_____

_____

_____

Respond to Reading

Answer the prompt below. Think about how the poet helps you understand the characters' feelings and points of view. Use your notes and graphic organizer.

How does the poet use words and phrases to help you understand how the characters in the poem feel about Ollie?

_____

_____

_____

_____

_____

_____

_____

_____

_____

_____

The Gentleman Bookworm

*Literature Anthology:
pages 500–501*

 How does the illustration help you understand the details in the poem?

 Talk About It Look at the illustration on pages 500 and 501. Talk with a partner about what the bookworms are doing.

Cite Text Evidence What clues in the illustration help you understand what the bookworms are doing? Write them in the chart.

 Synthesize Information

Use the illustration to help you understand the title of the poem. Look closely at the details about the main character and what he does to understand why the poet calls him a gentleman.

Illustration Clues	How It Helps

Write The poet uses the illustration to _____

_____

_____

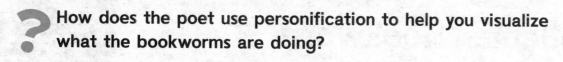

? **How does the poet use personification to help you visualize what the bookworms are doing?**

Talk About It With a partner, reread page 501. Talk about what the bookworms are doing that people usually do.

Cite Text Evidence What words and phrases describe things that people do? Write text evidence and tell how it helps you visualize.

Quick Tip

Take turns reading the poem aloud with a partner as the other acts out what the poem says. Miming the actions will help you visualize what the text is describing.

Text Evidence	What I Visualize

Write The poet uses personification in the poem by _____

_____

_____

Word Choice

Writers use word choice to create silly mental images to add humor to their writing. They may describe something as bigger, better, or worse than it actually is. They may also describe something impossible in order to create a funny mental image.

FIND TEXT EVIDENCE

*On page 501 of "The Gentleman Bookworm" in the **Literature Anthology**, the poet has the Gentleman Bookworm use the French expression "bon appétit," which is a way to wish that a guest enjoys the meal. By having a worm use an expression like this, the poet creates a mental image that is funny because it is something a gentleman would say, but a bookworm never could.*

> "Ah, *bon appétit!*"
> Cried the Gentleman Bookworm. "A toast!"

Your Turn Reread page 501.

- What are two more silly mental images that the poet includes?

  _____

  _____

- How do these mental images make the poem funny?

  _____

If you want your readers to laugh when they read what you write, choose descriptions that create silly mental images. Use comparisons that would be impossible in real life.

Text Connections

? How is the way poet Henry Leigh makes you feel similar to how the poets of "Ollie's Escape" and "The Gentleman Bookworm" make you feel?

Talk About It Read the excerpt from "The Twins." Talk with a partner about what is funny about the poem.

Cite Text Evidence Circle the words in the poem that rhyme. Underline what phrases are funny. Think about how the poet creates the tone or mood. Now think about how the other poems you read this week make you feel.

Write All three poets _____

_____

_____

_____

From
"The Twins"

In form and feature, face and limb,
　　I grew so like my brother,
That folks got taking me for him,
　　And each for one another.
It puzzled all our kith and kin,
　　It reach'd an awful pitch;
For one of us was born a twin,
　　Yet not a soul knew which.
One day (to make the matter worse),
　　Before our names were fix'd,
As we were being wash'd by nurse
We got completely mix'd.

　　　　　— Henry Leigh

Phrasing and Expression

Think about the tone of a poem when you read it aloud. Look at the punctuation and how the lines break. This is the poem's *phrasing*, or how words are organized. Understanding a poem's phrasing will help you to read with *expression*, or feeling.

Page 157

Ten flashlights clicked on to reveal,
That creepy crawly by my heel.

I blushed bright red, "Oops, I was wrong."
Snake?
No, a lizard—one-inch long.

The tone here is suspenseful and can be read in a mysterious voice.

The commas, question mark, and dash slow this part down by adding pauses.

> ## Quick Tip
>
> A humorous poem may include funny words or exaggerated reactions. As you read aloud, use exaggerated expressions during these parts to make the poem funny for your listeners.

Your Turn Turn to pages 158 and 159. Take turns reading "Bubble Gum" aloud with a partner. Think about the feelings being expressed, such as surprise. Express these feelings as you read the poem.

Afterward, think about how you did. Complete these sentences.

I remembered to _____

_____

Next time I will _____

_____

WRITING

Literature Anthology:
pages 496–498

Expert Model

Features of a Narrative Poem

A **narrative poem** is a kind of poetry. A narrative poem

- tells a story
- can have any number of lines and stanzas
- has rhythm and rhyme

Analyze an Expert Model Reread "Ollie's Escape" on pages 496–498 in the **Literature Anthology**. Use text evidence to answer the questions.

1 How does David Crawley use the lines and stanzas of his poem to tell a story?

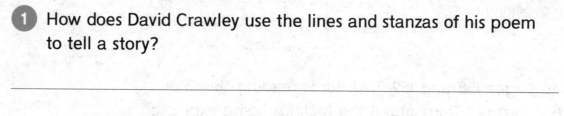

2 How does the poet help you visualize the main character, Ollie, in his poem?

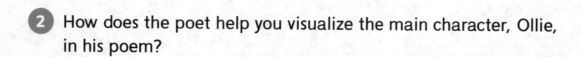

Word Wise

Writers use prepositions such as *before, after,* or *under* to describe a location of time or place. For example, David Crawley says, "He wiggled his way *toward* the teacher who jumped *on* her desk with a scream." The words *toward* and *on* describe the location of Ollie and the teacher.

Plan: Choose Your Topic

Brainstorm With a partner, think of a funny story that makes you laugh. It might be from a family trip, a time with friends at school, or a silly made-up tale. Use the sentence starters below to talk about your ideas.

> *Something that makes me laugh is . . .*
> *This story makes me laugh because . . .*

Writing Prompt Choose one of your story ideas to write a narrative poem.

I will write a poem about _____.

Purpose and Audience Think about your purpose for writing and who will read it.

How will you make your readers laugh as they read your poem?

_____

_____

_____

Plan Think about what happens in your story. Why do these events make you laugh? Who was there? Write three questions and answer them in your writer's notebook.

Plan: Ideas

Ideas Poets plan story ideas, such as characters and events, before they begin to write. They consider how the ideas can be organized into stanzas to tell the story.

Let's look at an expert model. Reread the beginning of "The Camping Trip."

> We roughed it at Old Piney Park,
>
> With tents and hot dogs after dark.
>
> I'd barely yawned and gone to sleep,
>
> When I felt something creep, creep, creep.

Think about the events described. Now reread the stanza and circle three things that happened at the beginning of the poem.

Think about your funny story. Talk with a partner about what happened. Use these sentence starters to plan the events:

> *The first thing that happened is . . .*
> *Next . . .*
> *Then . . .*

Chart In your writer's notebook, draw a Sequence chart. Fill in the chart to plan your writing. Be sure to write the events of your story in order.

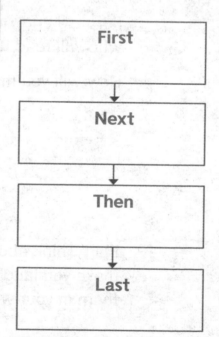

First

↓

Next

↓

Then

↓

Last

Draft

Rhythm and Rhyme Poets use rhythm and rhyme to give their poems a musical beat and tell a story in a fun and rhythmic way. Reread the first stanza of "The Gentleman Bookworm," on page 500 in the **Literature Anthology**. Use text evidence to answer the question.

How does J. Patrick Lewis use rhyming words to create a pattern?

_____

_____

Now use the first stanza on page 500 as a model to write what happens first in your narrative poem. Use rhyming words and rhythm to create a pattern.

_____

_____

_____

_____

_____

Write a Draft Look over your Sequence chart. Use it to help you write your draft in your writer's notebook. Remember to use your story ideas, as well as rhythm and rhyme.

Word Wise

Rhyming words sound the same, but they do not always look the same. Words with different spellings can still have the same sound. Look at these examples from the poem: Web, said; eat, *bon appétit*; rhyme, time.

Revise

Figurative Language Poets use figurative language, such as similes and onomatopoeia, to make their poems more fun to read. A simile compares two things using the words *like* or *as*. Onomatopoeia is using words that sound like what they mean.

Read these lines from a poem below. Then revise them so that they are more fun to read. Add figurative language.

The carnival came when I was ten,

I went two times then went home.

The rides were loud,

I had so much fun.

_____

_____

_____

_____

Revise Revise your draft. Check that the events are in the order they happened. Be sure you use figurative language and humor.

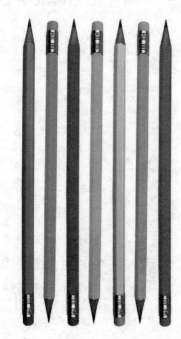

Peer Conferences

Review a Draft Listen carefully as a partner reads his or her draft aloud. Tell what you like about the draft. Use these sentence starters to help you discuss your partner's draft.

I like this part of the poem because . . .

You can use rhyme and rhythm here to . . .

Try using figurative language to describe . . .

I have a question about . . .

Partner Feedback After you take turns giving each other feedback, write one of the suggestions from your partner that you will use in your revision.

_____

_____

_____

_____

Revision After you finish your peer conference, use the Revising Checklist to help you make your narrative poem better. Remember to use the rubric on page 183 to help you with your revision.

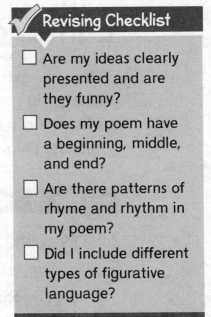

Revising Checklist

☐ Are my ideas clearly presented and are they funny?

☐ Does my poem have a beginning, middle, and end?

☐ Are there patterns of rhyme and rhythm in my poem?

☐ Did I include different types of figurative language?

Tech Tip

When you write your draft on a computer, you have the ability to move your lines easily. By using the cut and paste feature, you can put scrambled story events into sequential order.

Edit and Proofread

After you revise your narrative poem, proofread it to find any mistakes in grammar, spelling, and punctuation. Read your draft at least three times. This will help you catch any mistakes. Use the checklist below to edit your poem.

✔ Editing Checklist

- ☐ Do all lines begin with a capital letter?
- ☐ Is there a line break between stanzas?
- ☐ Are prepositions used to describe a location of time or place?
- ☐ Are all words spelled correctly?

List two mistakes that you found as you proofread your narrative poem.

_____

_____

_____

_____

_____

_____

Publish, Present, and Evaluate

Publishing When you publish your writing, you create a neat final copy that is free of mistakes. Write legibly in print or cursive, or type your final copy on a computer.

Presentation When you are ready to present, practice your presentation. Use the presenting checklist.

Evaluate After you publish, use the rubric to evaluate it.

1 What did you do successfully? _____

_____

2 What needs more work? _____

_____

_____

Presenting Checklist

☐ Look at your audience.

☐ Speak loudly and clearly.

☐ Use expression to convey the humor in your poem.

☐ Emphasize your rhythm and rhymes.

☐ Pause when your audience laughs.

4	3	2	1
• excellent use of figurative language • excellent use of rhyme and rhythm • very few spelling, grammar, or punctuation errors	• good use of figurative language • good use of rhyme and rhythm • some spelling, grammar, or punctuation errors	• some use of figurative language • some use of rhyme and rhythm • several spelling, grammar, and punctuation errors	• no use of figurative language • no use of rhyme and rhythm • many spelling, grammar, and punctuation errors

Read the selection and choose the best answer to each question.

Watching the Stars: The Story of Maria Mitchell

[1] A small streak in the sky might not seem like much, but on October 1, 1847, Maria Mitchell recognized that blurry streak in her telescope as a brand-new comet. Mitchell was unknown at the time, and might have stayed unknown. There were no recognized female astronomers. Many leading scientists might have ignored her contributions, but today, she is recognized as the first female astronomer. How was she able to overcome such a huge obstacle? She worked hard and had an important supporter—her father.

[2] Maria Mitchell was born on August 1, 1818. Her love of astronomy started in her childhood. Mitchell's father was a teacher and an astronomer. He made sure that all his children received the same education. This was unusual at the time. Most families only educated boys. Mitchell's father taught her how to use their family's telescope. She studied hard and followed in his footsteps. She spent every clear night she could observing the night sky.

[3]   After Mitchell graduated, she worked as a librarian for 20 years. She worked all day among books, and then spent her evenings among the stars. On that night in October 1847, Mitchell noted her discovery and ran to tell her father. He announced the news of her discovery to the scientific community.

[4]   Mitchell's discovery made her famous around the world. She became the first woman to be elected to the American Academy of Arts and Sciences. She toured the world and met scientists. Many women's groups celebrated her success. In 1865, she became a professor at Vassar Female College. She was the first female professor of astronomy in the country. She was also a pioneer in the study of sunspots.

[5]   Mitchell was an inspiration to her students. They often asked, "Did you learn that from a book, or did you observe it yourself?" She led her students in direct observations of solar eclipses.

[6]   Maria Mitchell died in 1889, but her legacy is celebrated even today. Her research and observations brought us all a little closer to the stars.

1 What problem is described in paragraph 1?

   A Maria Mitchell saw a mysterious light in the sky.

   B Maria Mitchell was an unknown female astronomer.

   C Maria Mitchell worked hard and had her father's support.

   D Many leading scientists ignored her contributions to astronomy.

2 The word *telescope* contains two Greek root words. The root *tele* means "far." What do you think the root *scope* means? —

   F space

   G distance

   H to travel

   J to look at

3 Reread paragraph 2. What did Mitchell's father do that was unusual?

   A He was a teacher and an astronomer.

   B He taught his children about astronomy.

   C He studied the night sky with a telescope.

   D He made sure all his children were educated.

Quick Tip
To choose the correct answer, reread the passage each question refers to. Look for words used in the answer choices in the text.

4 What is the theme, or main message, of "Watching the Stars: The Story of Maria Mitchell"?

   F Maria Mitchell became famous for discovering a comet.

   G The history of astronomy is an interesting one.

   H Hard work can help you overcome tough obstacles.

   J More women should become astronomers.

Read the selection and choose the best answer to each question.

The Memory Box

1 My mother set a giant box right in front of me.
She pointed to the box and said, quite casually,
"It's time to sort what to keep and throw away."
There were better ways I'd planned to spend my day.

2 It was spring cleaning time and she was on a spree,
But what, exactly, did that have to do with me?
She answered, "This is your cluttered closet's mess,
Stacks of stuff, and it's time to make it less."

3 She turned away, and I sat staring at my things.
Every piece, every paper and all those knotted strings
Meant something special that I didn't want to lose!
Please, I begged, do not make me choose!

4 This picture, for example, is not just a rainbow fern.
It took weeks to find the leaves to make the colors turn.
Dad and I tromped all over, searching high and low,
To perfect the pattern from deep red to bright yellow.

5 These pages here show how I learned to draw a perfect cat,
With ears up here and tail down there, and this jaunty little hat.
I never would have learned if I hadn't struggled then,
And I like to see the progress I made from four to ten.

6 "I'll tell you what," Mom said to me after a moment's pause,
"We'll make a memory book and track each memory's cause.
It'll clear the space up nicely without losing all your things,
The value isn't in this box, but in the memories it brings."

7 So, we sorted all my work from every age,
I told her each memory as I wrote it on the page.
Soon the box was empty and the closet space was clear,
And I had something better that I could always hold dear.

1 What is the root word of the word *casually* in stanza 1?

A casual

B casu

C usually

D casually

2 In stanza 4, what does the idiom *searching high and low* mean?

F searching in trees and on the ground

G searching everywhere

H searching in a few places

J searching on tippy-toes and kneeling

3 What do the two images on pages 187–188 help readers predict?

A that the poem will be about spring

B that the poem will be about cleaning

C that the poem will be about organizing memories

D that the poem will be about a box of things

4 How does the narrator of "The Memory Box" feel about cleaning out her closet?

F Exited to get started

G Scared about losing her things

H Annoyed at her mother

J Unsure about where to begin

> **Quick Tip**
>
> This poem is written in the first person, or from the point of view of the narrator. To understand that point of view, look for punctuation that expresses strong feeling.

COMPARING GENRES

- In the **Literature Anthology**, reread the drama "King Midas and the Golden Touch" on pages 476–489 and the narrative poem "Ollie's Escape" on pages 496–498.

- Use the Venn Diagram below to show how the two genres are the same and different.

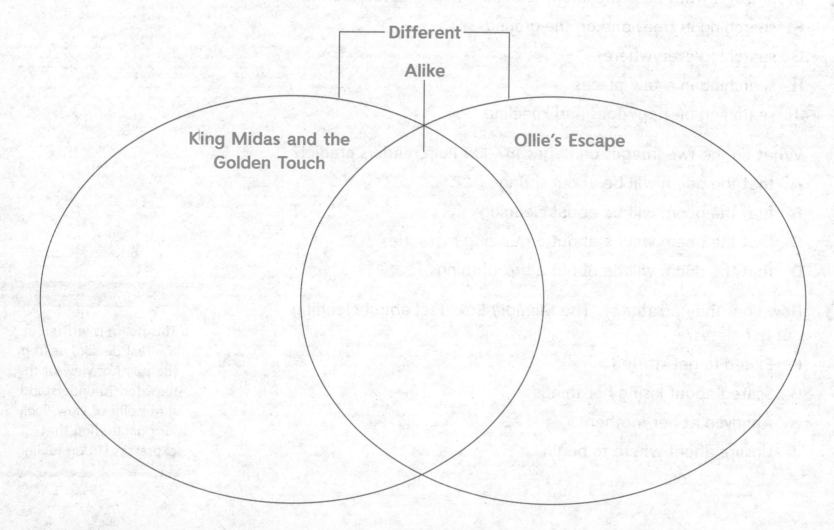

Different

Alike

King Midas and the Golden Touch

Ollie's Escape

IDIOMS

COLLABORATE

An idiom is a group of words that means something different from the usual meaning of each word in it. You can use context clues to help you figure out the meaning of an idiom.

> We were enjoying a quiet evening at home when suddenly the doorbell rang *out of the blue*.

The context clues *a quiet evening at home* and *suddenly* help readers figure out that the idiom *out of the blue* means "something that happens unexpectedly."

Read the sentences below. **Underline** context clues that help you figure out the meaning of the idiom. Then, write what it means.

The detective headed home disappointed. He'd been *barking up the*

wrong tree all day. _____

_____

Yasmin decided to *hit the sack* early after a long day of soccer

practice. _____

_____

_____

WRITE A PARAGRAPH

When you compare things, you look at how they're alike and different.

- Choose two heroes to compare and research their deeds.

- Think about how to present what you learned. Choose a genre such as biography, informational text, or opinion.

- In your chosen genre, write a paragraph that identifies and compares the deeds of both heroes.

The two heroes I chose to compare are _____

A heroic deed I read about was _____

WRITE A HEADLINE

A headline is the first part of an article. It is set in large type and states what readers are about to read.

- Research a new technology that could change people's lives.

- Write a headline for an article about the new technology. In the headline, state how the technology might affect readers.

The technology I researched was _____

Something I learned while researching was _____

_____

LIFE BOATS

Log on to **my.mheducation.com** and reread the online article "Life Boats," including the information found in the interactive elements. Answer the questions below.

Time for Kids: "Life Boats"

- Look at the map and use the map scale. About how far is Dhaka from Chittagong in kilometers?

  _____

  _____

- How has Rezwan used boats to adapt to his environment?

  _____

  _____

  _____

- Look at the chart, "Top 5 Rainiest Cities in the United States." What is the difference in inches between the rainfall in Mobile, Alabama, and the rainfall in New Orleans, Louisiana?

  _____

  _____

WHAT DID YOU LEARN?

Use the rubric to evaluate yourself on the skills that you learned in this unit. Write your scores in the boxes below.

4	3	2	1
I can successfully identify all examples of this skill.	I can identify most examples of this skill.	I can identify a few examples of this skill.	I need to work on this skill more.

☐ Point of View   ☐ Problem and Solution   ☐ Theme

☐ Root Words   ☐ Greek and Latin Roots   ☐ Idioms

Something I need to work more on is _____ because

_____

_____

_____

Text-to-Self Think back over the texts that you have read in this unit. Choose one text and write a short paragraph explaining a personal connection that you have made to the text.

I made a personal connection to _____ because _____

_____

_____

Present Your Work

COLLABORATE

Discuss how you will present your tall tale to the class. You might want to include funny illustrations of the hyperboles you used. Use the presenting checklist as you practice your presentation. Discuss the sentence starters below and write your answers.

Before I present, I will think about what parts to emphasize:

_____

_____

I think my presentation was _____

_____

✓ **Presenting Checklist**

☐ I will practice reading my tall tale aloud.

☐ I will speak loudly enough.

☐ I will use my voice to express the humor in my tall tale.

☐ I will pause if my audience is laughing.